PLAYING CARDS

ROGER TILLEY

 OCTOPUS

OCTOPUS BOOKS

ACKNOWLEDGMENTS

The author and publishers are grateful to the British Museum for permission to reproduce the majority of the playing cards illustrated, which were specially photographed by the Museum staff in the Department of Prints and Drawings, the Manuscript Room and the Thomas de la Rue and Co. Collection (housed in the British Museum). They are also grateful to the following for permission to reproduce the following illustrations: The Worshipful Company of Makers of Playing Cards, figs. 16, 53, 55 (photographed at the Guildhall Library by Derrick Witty); the National Portrait Gallery, fig. 34.

We are indebted to the following for permission to quote copyright material: *Biometrica* and Professor M. G. Kendall for the extract on page 15 from 'Studies in the History of Probability and Statistics'; Thames and Hudson Ltd for the extract on page 22 from *The Rise of Christian Europe* by Hugh Trevor-Roper (1966); to the Oxford University Press for a passage on page 28 from *Art and Civilization* (1928), arranged and edited by F. S. Marvin and A. F. Clutton-Brock for the Unity Series VIII; Houghton Mifflin Company for permission to quote the passage on page 74 from *A History of Playing Cards* by Catherine Perry Hargrave (1930); the Cambridge University Press for the piece from *The Mediaeval Manichee* by Professor Sir Steven Runciman (1947) on page 26.

This edition first published 1973 by
Octopus Books Limited
59 Grosvenor Street, London W 1

ISBN 0 7064 0049 6

© 1967 by George Weidenfeld & Nicolson Ltd

Produced by Mandarin Publishers Limited
77a Marble Road, North Point, Hong Kong
and printed in Hong Kong

Typeset in Hong Kong by
Asco Trade Typesetting Ltd

(preceding page)
Two cards from an Austrian pack of *c.* 1750;
hand-tinted woodcuts.

CONTENTS

A DETAILED ACCOUNT OF PLAYING CARDS would need many volumes. Cards are of old and mixed descent; their foresides bear many varying devices, they have many more uses than gaming and are known throughout the world. Gaily clad, the kings and queens and knights have had their portraits painted by miniaturists of imagination and talent. The numbered, or pip, cards have been drawn and decorated by designers of distinction. Packs illustrate social history and the history of costume; they touch on politics and religion, picture wars and revolutions. They enter castles, cottages and tents, railway-carriages and fortune-telling booths. For centuries they have enriched the card-sharper and impoverished the simpleton. Robert Greene, in his *Notable Discovery of Coosnage*, published in 1591, gives a vivid account of the fleecing of a countryman. 'There be requisite effectually to act the Art of cony-catching, three several parties; the Setter, the Verser and the Barnackle', and he goes on to explain how the three rogues induce the cony, that is the gull or pigeon, to take part in a game of cards. 'What will you play at?' asks the Barnackle, 'at Primero, Primo visto, Sant, one-and-thirty, new cut, or what shall be the game?' The Verser's proposal 'I will play with you at a game wherein can be no deceit, it is called mum-chance at cardes,' is readily agreed, and in the end the countryman finds himself stripped of the money in his purse, 'his rings if he have any, his sword, his cloke, or els what he hath about him' and 'with a cold humour unto his heart...he, his wife, his children, and his familie, are brought to extream miserie.'

So rich a history, so vast an area of illustration, require a profusion of packs, and the need has been met in abundance. Although in a short book bounds must be set and selection becomes imperative, much of the exuberance has been retained in the following pages. In the history, or evolution, of the four-suited pack, traced in the first six chapters, reference is made, in text or illustration, to many a famous pack, hand-painted or printed, engraved on wood, copper or steel. The special purpose packs, commemorative, satirical, geographical, historical, Biblical, astronomical and so on, are grouped together in the last chapter. This may mean that they do not take their places in the right sequence of time and country, but this is of small importance as they have had little or no effect on the development

2 *Das Biquet Spiel*, an engraving after J. E. Nilson.

1 *(opposite)* The ace of spades and six of coins from a pack made in Java by a native artist working in watercolour.

5

of the four-suited pack as we know it to-day. Their very
originality, unusual charm, and burden of information are
much too distracting to the eye and mind to allow of serious play.
Nor were they intended for that purpose. By separating them
from the others the main story is left uncluttered and they can be
considered, and enjoyed, for their own worth. It may well be
that history is compounded of the commonplace; but the
abnormal is usually more interesting.

3 *Das Lombre Spiel*, one of a series of engravings
after paintings by Johann Esaias Nilson, the
miniaturist, painter and engraver (1721–88).

THEORIES OF THE ORIGIN of playing cards are many in number, seldom probable, occasionally romantic and never capable of proof. Several look to the 'mysterious East' for the birth-place, only to stumble on the twin stones of the equally obscure 'Mysterious People', the gypsies, and the absence of any oriental card even distantly resembling the kind in which we are interested. As for the 'Mysterious People', the East-centred speculations normally attribute to the gypsies the bringing of cards from East to West. Alas for such ideas; for whilst it is not now doubted that the original home of the gypsies was some part, as yet unidentified, of India, they were first heard of in Bohemia in 1398, Basle in 1414, Rome in 1422 and Barcelona in 1427, and by the earliest of these dates cards were firmly established in Europe. As Mark Twain said of science, 'one gets such wholesale returns of conjecture out of a small investment of fact.'

The leading exponent of the Eastern theory, Dr Stewart Culin, Director of the Brooklyn Museum, writing in 1895, and leaning heavily on W.G. Wilkinson of the British China Consular Service, maintains that both chess and cards are in direct descent from the Korean divinatory arrow. Dr Culin quotes a manuscript prepared by Mr Wilkinson for publication in the Korean Repository:

The heart-shaped scroll on the back of the cards, however, reveals their true significance. This mark is a survival of one of the feathers of the arrow from which they were derived. Mr Cushing had suggested to me that the numerals are also derived from feathers, being survivals of the cut cock-feathers of the original arrow... As to the forms of the cards, they are clearly copied from slips of bamboo, such as are used as divining lots at the present day in China. In fact an almost exact replica of the Korean pack is to be found in the eighty consecutively numbered lots, *ts im*, used by Chinese gamblers to divine the lucky numbers in the lottery called *Pák Kòp pui*. The latter retain the arrowlike tip, while the cards bear the arrow features and the names of both are almost identical with that of arrow, *tsin*.

At an unknown time 'in or before the twelfth century', and through an equally unknown agency, the divinatory arrow of Korea and the paper money of China were brought together; for Chinese playing cards, writes Dr Culin, 'are derived from paper notes which bore pictorial symbols of their values. These symbols furnished the suit-marks of the Chinese pack, and, copied again in Europe without knowledge of their true signifi-

4 King of hearts from de Brianville's *Jeu de Blason*, first published in 1658.

(following spread)
5 *(left)* Four hand-coloured *tarocchini* from a pack designed and etched by Guiseppe Maria Mitelli in the seventeenth-century.

6 *(right)* Four Hindu cards made from the lacquered scales of a fish. Early nineteenth-century. There are many variations in the suits of Indian cards and they are sometimes hard to identify.

7

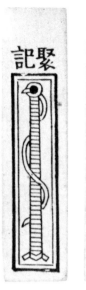
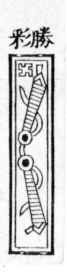

cance, gave rise to the coins, clubs, swords and cups of the European game.' The four suits in the cards of South China are coins, strings of coins, myriads of strings of coins and tens of myriads of strings of coins, with three extra cards. Both Korean and Chinese cards are narrow strips of paper varying from about $1\frac{1}{2}$ inches to nearly 8 inches in length and about $\frac{3}{8}$ inches to $1\frac{1}{2}$ inches in width [figure 8].

The four suits and the value-marked cards, considered in conjunction with the discovery by the Chinese of paper and woodblock printing, make cogent arguments in support of this theory. Yet, leaving aside the two problems of migration to the West and the total difference in appearance, there is the difficulty that no normally faced Chinese card earlier than the eighteenth century has yet come to light.

One of the more romantic legends asserts that playing cards were invented in China in AD 1120 to provide amusement for the Emperor Sèun-ho's concubines. India, not to be outdone in romance or originality, has a tradition that cards were devised by the favourite, and obviously highly-strung, wife of a Maharajah to wean him from the irritating habit of pulling his beard. A better, though not entirely convincing, reason for recognizing India as the cradle of cards is that Ardhanari, a composite god, the left half being Siva the destroyer god and the right half his spouse, Devi, whose attributes are obscure, is always depicted with Siva holding in his two hands a cup and a wand and Devi a sword and ring in hers; it is urged that the remarkable resemblance between these emblems and the cup, sword, coin and baton suit-marks of the early European packs is proof enough. Better still, Hanuman, the monkey god, a child of a nymph and the wine god, holds in four of his hands a cup, a sword, a ring and a sceptre.

Unhappily there is no likeness between Indian and European cards, or, for that matter, between Ardhanari's emblems and Indian cards. Indeed Indian cards are entirely different from those of any other country. They are circular, made from thin discs of wood, tortoiseshell, canvas, ivory or even fish scales, heavily lacquered, enamelled and hand-painted [figure 6]. There are eight or ten suits in a set of Indian cards, each suit having twelve cards. The ten suits illustrate the ten reincarnations of Vishnu the preserver god, in the first nine of which he has rescued the world from various perils such as the giant Hiranyscopa and the dwarf Vamanatara, and in the tenth of which, yet to come, he will finally overcome the powers of evil. The differences between European and Indian cards are too great to make the theory of an Indian origin acceptable, and in the absence of any documentary or material evidence of western-type playing cards being found in India before the sixteenth century, Dr Eberhard Pinder (a leading modern authority and

8 Six Chinese cards, two from each of the suits of coins, strings of coins and myriads of strings of coins (nineteenth-century).

7 (opposite) Das Pharo Spiel, an engraving after J. E. Nilson.

11

9 The twenty-two *tarocchi* or triumphs which complete the tarot pack, the whole forming the Tarot. The French names, oddly enough more widely used than the original Italian, are Le Mat or Le Fol (The Fool); Le Bateleur (The Illusionist); La Papesse (The Popess); L'Impératrice (The Empress); L'Empereur (The Emperor); Le Pape (The Pope); L'Amoureux (The Lovers); Le Chariot (The Chariot); La Roue de Fortune (Wheel of Fortune); La Force (Force); Le Pendu (The Hanging Man); [no title] (Death); La Tempérance (Temperance); Le Diable (The Devil); La Maison de Dieu (The Tower); L'Étoile (The Star); La Lune (The Moon); Le Soleil (The Sun); Le Jugement (The Judgment); Le Monde (The World).

Director for many years until his death in 1964 of the Deutsches Spielkarten Museum, Bielefeld, where there is a particularly important collection of Indian cards) agreed with Dr Culin that in all probability India first saw cards in the hands of Spanish or Portuguese seamen.

The supporters of the Indian theory have produced two picturesque alternatives to the gypsies as bearers of playing cards from East to West. The first holds the Crusaders responsible, largely because Godfrey of Bouillon, on his return from the First Crusade, brought with him chess, which had reached the Holy Land from India. It is further suggested that originally Indian cards were used on the chessboard instead of the usual chessmen. The second turns to the opposite camp and burdens the Saracens with the responsibility of transference. The foundation of this story is that the Italian and Spanish words for cards, *naipes* and *naibi* respectively, closely resemble the Arabic word *naib*. On the other hand the Moors were not ousted

from Spain until 1492, by which time cards had been known in Europe for more than a hundred years, giving plenty of time for an Arabic word to be used to describe a European invention.

The claims of Persia are not so strenuously advanced as those of China and India, and to all intents and purposes rest on the point that poker is derived from the ancient Persian game of *âs-nâs*. This seems a narrow base for so broad a claim. Persian cards are square and of beautiful workmanship.

The pretensions of India and Persia cannot be dismissed without consideration of the possibility that the first card games were derived from chess. Although its own origins have been much disputed, it is generally accepted that chess has for its immediate forerunner a fifth-century Persian game called *shah-mat,* a changeling for a game played in India from remote times under the name of *chaturanga*. This game, its name derived from the Sanskrit *chatur* (four) and *anga* (a member of an army), required four players, two being allied against two.

13

Clearly there is a resemblance between the four-handed game of chess and the four-suited game of cards. Mere similarity, however, is a weak argument on which to found a strong case, and the weakness is emphasized by the further reasoning that chess, a game in which the toss-up for the opening move is the sole element of chance, and in which all the pieces are fully exposed, cannot be the forerunner of any game where luck is predominant and the pieces undisclosed. Against this it is argued that chess is a war game with sets of men attacking, defending and taking prisoners like hostile armies, and that

10 Four cards from a pack printed by Chas. Goodall & Son to commemorate the Diamond Jubilee of Queen Victoria in 1897.

card-games can be seen as an improved version, since in real war the composition of an army is unknown to its enemies and luck enters into its operations. Incidentally, the Korean word for cards, *Htou-tjyen,* might be translated as 'fighting tablets'. At this point one cannot help wondering if it were the demands of chivalry which prompted the omission of the queen from some of the early packs; for only in the last half century has it been thought fit and proper for women to don uniform and become subservient to military command.

The moves in *chaturanga* are made according to the throws of an oblong, four-sided die, and dice have their own supporters as the claimants to the honourable title we seek to bestow. Their case rests partly on their great antiquity and partly on the striking similarity between the number of cards, fifty-six, in the early packs and the number of ways, also fifty-six excluding permutations, in which three dice can be thrown. The argument, however, is difficult to sustain in view of the point made by Professor M.G. Kendall: 'Up to the fifteenth century we find few traces of a probability calculus and, indeed, little to suggest the emergence of the idea that a calculus of dice-falls was necessary.'

Since there is no conclusive evidence that the origin of cards is to be found in the East it seems possible, even probable, that they are the product of European genius; and there has been much furious argument as to which European country shall have the honours of invention. The candidates are:

Italy, with suit-signs of *spadi, battoni, coppe* and *denari* (swords, clubs, cups and coins)

Germany, with suit-signs of *eicheln, blatt* or *grün, herzen* and *schellen* (acorns, leaves, hearts and bells)

France, with suit-signs of *trèfles, piques, coeurs* and *carreaux* (clubs, spades, hearts and diamonds).

No absolute proof can be given of the place or time of their arrival on the European scene, though help with the date is given by the following negative evidence:

1363. Playing cards are not mentioned in instructions to clerics issued by the Abbé of St Germain proscribing all games of dice or chance under the penalty of deprivation of wine for one week.

1369. Playing cards are not mentioned in a decree against gaming issued by Charlies V.

1375. Playing cards are not referred to by Petrarch (1304–74) or his friend Boccaccio (1313–75), although they mention other pastimes and instruments of gambling.

Hitherto the history of playing cards seems to have been a matter of speculation and ingenious supposition, of questions rather than answers. It is, therefore, both a relief and an encouragement to meet the first established fact. The date is 1377.

(following spread)

11 *(left)* Six cards from a Spanish pack printed in Madrid in the first quarter of the nineteenth century.

12 *(right)* Eight cards engraved by Don José Martinez de Castro in 1810, hand-painted and published in Madrid.

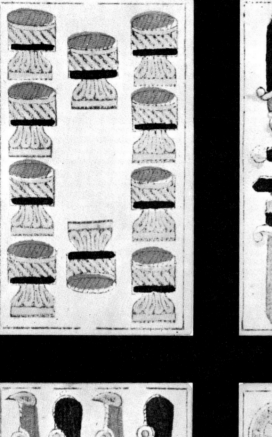

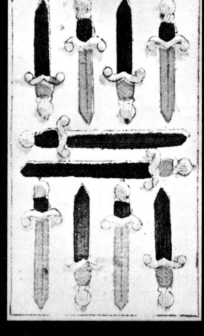

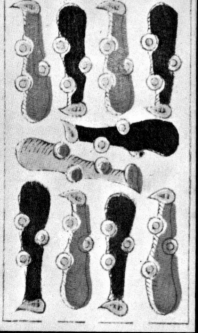

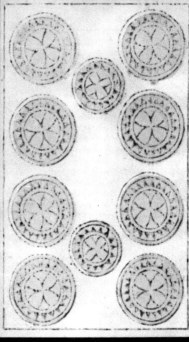

THE ITALIAN AND SPANISH PACKS

THE EARLIEST KNOWN ORIGINAL DOCUMENT with an unarguable reference to playing cards is a manuscript, dated 1377, written in Latin by a German monk living in a Swiss monastery and preserved by the British Museum [figure 15]. It is certainly interesting, if not significant, that thereafter references to cards become increasingly frequent. In 1378 cards were prohibited in the German city of Regensburg; in 1379 the accounts of the Dukedom of Brabant record the payment of '4 peters, 2 florins, value $8\frac{1}{2}$ moutons' for the purchase of *speelquarten;* and in 1380 playing cards are mentioned in the *Pflichtbuch* of Nuremberg. Earlier works mentioning playing cards lack the authority of the original manuscript and the references in the copies available are thought to be interpolations by later editors or transcribers.

Shortly after the 1377 manuscript came into the possession of the British Museum it was reported on by Mr E.A. (later Sir Edward) Bond, the Principal Librarian, in the *Athenaeum* of 19 January 1878, No. 2621, and the following passages are taken from that report.

In his Prologue, the author gives his name as *Johannes, in ordine praedicatorum minimus, nacione Theutonicus.* He prefaces his statement by an argument that . . . Heaven not only disposes and prepares things on earth for the reception of its impressions, but ordains instruments or games by which they may be signified. Then he proceeds: 'Hence it is that a certain game called the game of cards *(ludus cartarum),* has come to us in this year, viz the year of our Lord M.CCC.L.XXVIJ. In which game the state of the world as it now is is excellently described and figured. But at what time it was invented, where, and by whom I am entirely ignorant . . . But the subject of this treatise may be compared with the game of chess, for in both these are kings, queens and chief nobles, and common people, so that both games may be treated in a moral sense.

'And in this treatise I propose to do three things: first, to describe the game of cards in itself, as to the matter and mode of playing it; second, to moralize the game, or teach noblemen the rule of life; and third, to instruct the people themselves, or inform them of the way of labouring virtuously. Wherefore it seemed to me that the present treatise ought to be entitled 'De Moribus et Disciplina Humane Conversationis'. For the first part will have six chapters. In the first will be stated the subject of the game and the diversity of instruments. In the second will be set forth that in this game there is a moral action of the virtues and vices. In the third it will be suggested that it is of service for mental relief and rest to the tired. In the fourth it will be shown that it is useful for idle persons, and may be a comfort to them. In the fifth will be treated the state of the world, as it is, in respect to morals. In the sixth will be demonstrated the aliquot parts of the number sixty, and the properties of numbers.'

14 Card engraved on steel, hand-painted, from a *minchiate* pack *c.* 1750. The folded back-paper, intended to strengthen the edges, is frequently seen in early Italian cards.

13 *(opposite)* Four cards illustrating the Spanish suit-signs. They are the same as the Italian, but the design and arrangement are much clearer.

The first chapter treats *de materia ludi et de diversitate instrumentorum*, and contains all that directly bears upon the game. It is as follows:

'In the game which men call the game of cards they paint the cards in different manners, and they play with them in one way and another. For the common form and as it came to us is thus, viz, four kings are depicted on four cards, each of whom sits on a royal throne. And each one holds a certain sign in his hand, of which signs some are reputed good, but others signify evil. Under which kings are two "marschalli", the first of whom holds the sign upwards in his hand, in the same manner as the king; but the other holds the same side downwards in his hand. After this there are other ten cards, outwardly of the same size and shape, on the first of which the aforesaid king's sign is placed once; on the second twice; and so on with the others up to the tenth card inclusive. And so each king becomes the thirteenth, and there will be altogether fifty-two cards. Then there are others who in the same manner play, or make, the game of queens, and with as many cards as has been already said of the kings. There are also others who so dispose the cards or the game that there are two kings, with their "marschalli" and other cards, and two queens with theirs in the same manner. Again, some take five, others six kings, each with his "marschalli" and his other cards, according as it pleases them, and thus the game is varied in form by many. Also, there are some who make the game with four kings and eight "marschalli" and the other common cards, and add besides four queens with four attendants, so that each of those four kings, with all the family of the whole kingdom, speaking of the chief persons, is there, and the number of the cards will then be sixty...'

Unfortunately the holy friar is so fascinated with his view of the game that in the remainder of his work he omits to describe the various methods of playing it.

At the end of the treatise is a note implying that the MS was copied in 1472, and a duplication in the Imperial Library at Vienna, so rich in incunabula, was noted by Denis, who described it in his catalogue of 1793–1802.

From this notable account of his spiritual reflections and

15 A page from the MS by the monk Johannes. The date can be seen in the left-hand column.

16 *(opposite)* The ace of spades from a fifteenth-century tarot pack, painted in colour on vellum and enriched with a kind of gold gesso. Possibly from the pack recorded by Domenico Bordigallo, in *Annals of Cremona*, as being painted by Antonio di Cicognara in 1484.

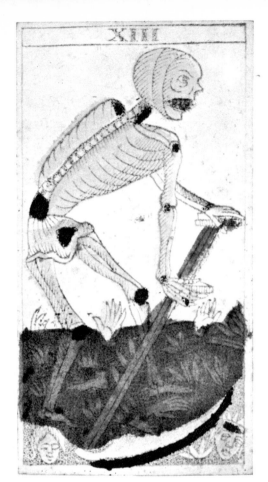

educational intentions it is clear that Johannes knew of at least six different card games. Although it is, nowadays, a long and fearsome task to invent a new game – it is said to have taken four or five years to perfect canasta – it may well have been a simpler, quicker business when they were still a novelty. Whatever the period of invention, cards can scarcely have appeared later than 1370, and probably earlier. It is reasonable to presume that Boccaccio and Petrarch were not entirely up-to-date in the closing years of their lives and that Johannes, in the seclusion of his monastery, was not acquainted with all card games.

Johannes does not describe the signs on the cards he saw; but if they were of Italian origin, and Italy, with Ferrara (on the stylistic grounds of the proportion of background to figure) as the most likely city, is thought to have ushered in the European pack, then the suit-marks would have been swords, curved and interlaced, cups or chalices, coins and batons [figure 21]. In these emblems some philosophers have detected the classes into which society was divided, swords standing for the knightly or aristocratic class, chalices for the Church, coins for the merchants or middle class, and clubs for the peasants or soldiery. Others see the emblems of four of the virtues, namely the sword of justice, the club or mace of fortitude, the coin of charity and the cup or chalice of faith; and a third group, the enemies of card-playing, see in the same signs the swords and clubs of violence, the coins of extravagance, and the cups of drunkenness.

It is noteworthy that Johannes speaks only of kings and queens and marshals and numbered cards. He does not so much as hint at the twenty-two cards with bizarre designs associated with the tarot pack [figures 9 and 17]. Nearly fifty years later St Bernardine of Siena, ('whose sour puritan face', Professor Trevor-Roper tells us, 'stares at us from so many Umbrian churches'), in his famous sermon at Bologna in 1423, denouncing cards equally with dice, notes the four suits and mentions the court cards; but he makes no reference to any other parts of the pack. Yet another forty or fifty years must pass before the strange devices creep into print, and then another sermon of about 1450–70 (written by a Franciscan Friar in Northern Italy and described at a meeting of the Society of Antiquaries on 31 May 1900 by Mr Robert Steele FSA) denounces dice, cards and triumphs as instruments of gambling, and clearly distinguishes between the four-suited pack and the twenty-two cards variously called tarots or *tarocchi* or *attuti* or *trionfi* in Italy and *atouts* in France on the grounds that they triumph over all other cards.

From the premises provided by the treatise and sermons it can be safely argued that cards first appeared in Europe in about 1370; that the original pack consisted of fifty-two cards; that in about 1470 the tarots appeared as a distinct entity; and that at a later date the two sequences were married to form the tarot

17 Death, whose scythe the severed head and hands apparently survive.

The king and queen of cups from an early
teenth-century woodcut pack with couble-
d triumphs as well as court cards.

pack used for the game of *tarocchi* of Venice (with queen
to make seventy-eight – fifty-six plus twenty-two – ca
pack) *tarocchino* of Bologna (twos, threes, fours and fives
to make a pack of sixty-two) [figure 5], and *minchiate* of F
(requiring a ninety-six card pack achieved by addi
Cardinal and three Theological Virtues, the four Eleme
the twelve signs of the Zodiac). With the advent of *m*
the pack became far too cumbersome and the normal car
again separated.

We now reach the most difficult of all the many questions posed by playing card history. What is the meaning, or significance, of the tarots? Book after book has been written in support of every shade of opinion, ranging from derision to veneration, from the view that the cards are no more than the tools in trade of the charlatanic fortune-teller to the belief that with the Bible and the Great Pyramid they form the three supreme mysteries of all time.

Several considerations present themselves when trying to resolve the mystery of the Tarot. It is most unlikely that the original artist drew twenty-two designs at random – that is to say 'doodled'. Almost certainly he followed a theme, and since art cannot be divorced from the cultural climate of its time attention must be given to the ideas of the early Renaissance. What were the subjects of its art? The most frequent were Christian ideas, the holy persons of the Gospels and the legends of the saints. And in the late Romanesque and early Renaissance periods the pictorial arts were employed by the monks to help in the instruction of the great mass of people who could not read. Is it not, therefore, extremely likely that the 'Master of the Tarot' put into operation Johannes' grand design of using cards for teaching noblemen and instructing the people? And here it is worth noting that the celebrated *tarocchi* of Mantegna, which are neither *tarocchi*, nor cards, nor by Mantegna, were undoubtedly designed as a portable encyclopaedia of men, muses, arts, virtues and planets for the young noblemen of the time. Religious teaching granted, it is far from certain that the instruction of the Tarot was strictly in accordance with the tenets of orthodox Christianity.

On the one hand, Christian thought of the Middle Ages has been detected in much of the sequence. For example, the Hanging Man has been claimed as a representation of the Suffering God; in the alive appearance of the limbs and heads left by the scythe of Death [figure 17] can be seen the notion that death is not the last dead ditch of man's damnation but the furrow from which the soul shall rise anew; and in the Fool can be discerned the command to sell all that we have and give to the poor, the joy of following our private star unhampered by worldly possessions, and the satisfaction of being the raw material of other men's good works – the man to whom the Pastor preaches, the patient on whom doctors and nurses practise the noble art of medicine, the subject of the Good Samaritan's beneficence.

On the other hand, the author of the 1450 sermon, writing, so far as we know, at the time of the introduction of the Tarot, says:

Concerning the third class of games, that is "triumphs". There is nothing in the world of gaming so hateful to God as the game of "triumphs". For everything

RE DI DANARI

REG. DI BASTONI

CAVAL DI COPPE

REG. DI DANARI

that is base in the eyes of the Christian faith is seen in "triumphs", as will be evident when I run through them. For "triumphs" are said, so it is believed, to have been given their name by the Devil, their inventor, because in no other game does he triumph (with less of souls to boot) as much as in this one. In it not only are God, the angels, the planets, and the cardinal virtues represented and named, but also the world's luminaries, I mean the Pope and the Emperor, are forced, a thing which is ridiculous and degrading to Christians, to enter in the game. For there are 21 "triumphs" which are the 21 steps of a ladder which takes a man to the depths of Hell.

And in the next paragraph, in which he names the cards, his comment on the Popess is: 'Unhappy men – the Christian faith denies this', and on the Pope, 'O Pontiff, why, etc., he who ought to be esteemed in all holiness, even him these mockers make their own chief.'

It is difficult to reconcile the Christian traces in the Tarot with the bitter denunciation with which it is introduced to our attention. Perhaps the solution is to be found in the following remarks of Professor Sir Steven Runciman in *The Mediaeval Manichee, A Study of the Christian Dualist Heresy:*

The only Occultist product of Christian Dualism may lie, as I have suggested above, in the symbolism of the Tarot pack... There seems to me to be a trace of Dualism in the pack, but it has since been overlaid with debased Kabbalistic lore. It shows in the antithesis of the Emperor and the Empress on the one hand, and the Pope and the Priestess or Pope Joan on the other, in the traditional interpretation of the Devil as betokening natural forces – he is represented holding a naked man and woman in chains – and in the card betokening disaster, the Tower Struck by Lightning, or Maison Dieu, which suggests the heretic's view of a Catholic church. The Priestess is also reminiscent of the Gnosis – Goddess of the Gnostics. But the evidence is far too slight to allow of any definite pronouncement.

If the teaching were heretical it would provide an excellent reason for the Inquisition to root it out and suppress all trace, and would explain why no early interpretation of the Tarot has survived.

The tarots persist to this day, though in many cases they have degenerated into quite meaningless designs, mainly of natural history. The original forms are still in use in Southern France, Italy and Hungary. It is a moot point whether it is odder that the meaning of the cards has been lost despite their continued production for five hundred years or that for five hundred years they have been produced unchanged.

The first playing cards to be made in Europe were hand-painted, a luxury of great beauty confined to the upper classes and much favoured as presents, particularly wedding presents, among the rich nobles and princes. They were produced by professional painters who found patronage at the ducal courts. Among those who were specifically painters of playing cards at, for instance, Ferrara were Alessandro di Bartolome Quartesana, Don Domenico Messore, Giovanni de Lazzaro Cagnola and Petrecino of Florence. Their rewards were handsome. In 1415 Fillippe Maria Visconti, Duke of Milan, paid his secretary, Marziano (or Martino) de Tortone, 1500 *écus d'or* for the procurement of a single pack. However, as card-playing became more popular and the demand spread beyond the confines of court circles their production was stimulated and realized by the use of stencils. Sometimes the outlines were stencilled and then hand-tinted; sometimes the whole process was carried out with stencils, the uncut sheets of cards being passed round a table for each workman or workwoman to add a particular colour with the sweep of a broad brush. The price fell in consequence and playing cards soon became more generally available.

In these packs the kings have wide-brimmed hats which resemble the primitive Sign of Eternal Life, i.e. the figure 8 lying on its side. (*Il Bagatto* and *La Forza*, the first and eleventh cards of the Tarot, have similar hats.) A regal crown forms the hat crown, except in the case of the king of coins whose crown, most remarkably, is balanced on the edge of the hat brim, at the back. All the kings are seated, the king of coins in an informal, cross-legged pose, right leg over left; and he has a self-satisfied smile, no doubt arising from his successful balancing trick

20 *(opposite)* Four cards from a pack made in Milan *c.* 1530.

[figure 20]. All the queens are seated and crowned, though the queen of coins has, like her husband, a difficult task; for her crown is not atop but at the end of her head-dress, her hair being drawn backwards in a caul. As a rule, the queen of batons has a topless gown [figure 20]. Each chevalier is mounted and each knave afoot; all wear a hat or close-fitting cap, with the exception of the chevalier of cups who, normally, is as bare-headed as the queen of batons is bare-bosomed. Now and again he appears with a chaplet of leaves.

No sooner were cards produced in quantity than card-playing spread, despite the condemnation of the Church, whose saints and bishops, priests and deacons thundered from the pulpit and execrated this vice in the market square. Nor, as Eugene Kolb points out in *Regi Játékkártyár*, were their efforts of greater avail than those of their successors in the following century who denounced the vile habit of smoking. Only a few years after the introduction of tobacco plants by Jean Nicot, half Europe was smoking, despite secular taxation and ecclesiastical condemnation. It was the same with cards. Despite royal decree and religious denunciation, the whole of Europe took to card-playing. Card-painting guilds were formed, card-making became a profitable profession, and soon hardly a country was left in which cards were not manufactured.

Packs with the Italian suit-marks spread outwards to Spain, parts of Switzerland, South-west Germany, Austria, Bohemia, Poland and Provence, and it is interesting that they were not the first art-form to follow this trail; for as the veteran Professor Joseph Strzygowski of Vienna remarked at the seventh Unity History School in 1923: 'What we call Romanesque art has its first monuments in Southern France, the old Aquitaine, in Lombardy and on the banks of the Rhine.' The craft of card production not only followed art, as the squire followed his knight, from Italy into Spain, but on arrival it assumed the local colouring. Spanish cards are dressed in bright yellows, oranges, greens and blues, with little or no shading; and of Spanish pictures we are told in *Annals of The Artists of Spain*: 'moving southward we enter into fairer regions both in nature and in art. The tawny brown of the Castiles ... gives place to fields green and flowery, and mendicants flaunting in blue and scarlet rags ... vivid mulberry and violet hues brighten the canvases of Valencia and golden yellows enrich those of Seville.'

The Spaniards adopted the same suit-marks as the Italians – swords or *espadas*, coins or *oros*, batons or *bastos* and chalices or *copas* – but gave them clearer outlines and simpler arrangements. Instead of rapiers, the swords have become cutlasses, straight and set well apart either vertically or horizontally; and the batons have turned into stout, very knobbly cudgels, also separately displaced. Thus each card can be recognized im-

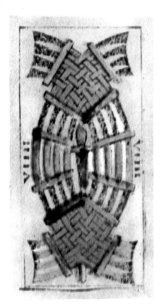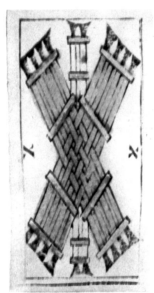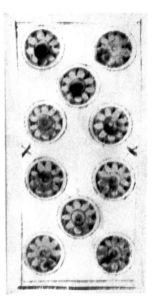

mediately; neither pause nor second glance is needed to count the number of batons or swords, wrapped in an indistinct bundle, or indeed to distinguish one from the other [figure 13].

Can it be doubted, artistry apart, that the Spanish arrangement is better than the Italian? And since an improvement cannot precede, must of necessity succeed, that which is improved upon, Spain must yield pride of place in chronology, though not necessarily in quality, to Italy. How cards ever reached Spain is as yet a question with no established answer. The best theory is that of M. d'Allemagne, who puts forward the knapsacks of the Papal troops who followed du Guesclin in his campaign of 1367 against Pedro the Cruel.

Suit-marks apart, Spanish cards have several interesting characteristics. Two of the aces have been picked out for special attention, that of *oros* normally displaying the arms of Spain and that of *espadas* a sword supported by a boy [figure 12]. Rather in the manner of the old-fashioned shop which exhibited both the proprietor's name and business in letters and the traditional sign of his calling, Spanish cards have a second method of indicating the suit; it is distinguished by the number of gaps in the top and bottom marginal lines, one gap for *copas*, two for *espadas* and three for *bastos*. The Spanish kings stand erect instead of being seated in the Italian style, are crowned and wear flowing robes normally trimmed with ermine. There is no queen, the court cards being king or *rey*, knight or *caballero* or *caballo* and knave or *sota*. The knights are mounted on spirited chargers and the knaves stand; both of them sometimes wear hats with graceful feathers and sometimes close-fitting caps [figures 11 and 12]. The king of money sometimes wears a sword; but he and his knight and knave and the court of chalices are generally un-

21 Four cards from an eighteenth-century pack showing the Italian suit-marks – cups, swords, coins and batons.

22, 23 The knave of cups and unarmed king of coins from a pack published by Llombart of Barcelona in 1815.

armed, presumably relying on their ability to buy off trouble in the one case and on the help of Providence in the other. The former are apt to have a deprecatory look and the latter a self-satisfied one.

The standard Spanish pack has no ten; and for the national game of *ombre* the eights and nines are also suppressed, making a pack of forty. The Tarot was, and is, quite unknown in Spain.

Cards of Spanish design were carried all over the world in the ships of Henry the Navigator, Bartholomew Diaz, Christopher Columbus, Vasco da Gama and many other less distinguished seamen. The sailors, soldiers and merchants aboard spent any time they could spare in gambling with cards. They took cards ashore and taught their games to the inhabitants, who copied the cards in their own style and using their own materials and their own draughtsmanship [figure 1]. Thus the so-called native packs of forty cards with Spanish, or Spanish-derived, suit-marks are found throughout the world from Central America to the Celebes, from North America to Goa. And the tradition has persisted throughout the centuries. In a booklet, *Apache Playing Cards*, the well-known American playing card historian, Mrs Virginia Wayland, comments on four Apache packs, hand-painted on skin, showing the traditional Spanish suit-marks crudely represented in the usual bright Spanish colours. Mrs Wayland has given these as recent a date as 1850–1900 [figure 53].

Unfortunately no very old Spanish cards have survived the erosion of time, perhaps because of the Spaniards' excessive passion for card-playing. A Flemish author who travelled through Spain in the first half of the fifteenth century particularly remarked on the way cards were to be found in every village, nay every cottage, however humble. Whether it be the result of fair wear and tear, or vandalism, or, simply, that few, if any, cards worthy of preservation were produced at an early date, no pack published before the year 1600 has yet come to light. Certainly a large proportion of Spanish cards were of indifferent quality, doubtless because the low price that they usually commanded prohibited quality in production; nevertheless several packs of exceptional quality were produced in Madrid at the beginning of the nineteenth century – at the time when Goya was at the height of his fame. Beautifully designed, finely engraved on copper and delicately coloured by hand, they reached the highest levels of card production.

THE GERMAN PACK

THE MANUFACTURE OF PLAYING CARDS with Italo-Spanish suitmarks followed a course no different from that of any other invention. The home trade secured, the product quickly moves outwards, obtaining a firm grip on the markets of neighbouring countries, and then seeks customers in distant fields. Next, competition is aroused, opposition met, and battle joined for commercial dominance. So it was with cards. As the new product spread to the West and North, Germany entered the lists against the original manufacturers, her strength as a competitor powerfully aided by her own introduction into Western Europe of the art of wood-engraving.

The development of wood-engraving was not only of immense commercial importance to Germany but drew the art and craft of card-making along the traditional routes of mediaeval art. Professor Strzygowski points out:

There are climatic reasons which explain why northern art starts from handicraft. The necessities of homebuilding and clothing gave a strong direction to the evolutionary process ... the south lived in caves and painted pictures on the walls ... the great amalgamation which formed mediaeval art came step by step, from south to north. The northern man ... pressed south [and] brought much and imbibed much of what he found .... The movement from south to north is a missionary one, not only in religion but in all humanistic wisdom.

Germany's first move in establishing her position as a card-manufacturing nation in her own right was to introduce suitmarks of her own design: hearts or *herzen*, bells or *schellen*, leaves or *grün* or *laub,* and acorns or *eicheln* [figure 27]. In these symbols it is less easy to discern the divisions of society espied in the Italian pack; but bells, that is to say hawk-bells, are sometimes said to indicate the knightly classes, hearts the Church, leaves the citizens and acorns the peasants. The true German sequence excludes the queen, her place being taken by a knave known as *obermann*, or colloquially *ober* [figure 27]. The original, now second, knave becomes the *untermann*, or *unter*, and the two, or *daus*, replaces the ace as the highest value card, making a pack of forty-eight. Until the beginning of the sixteenth century the ten is a single, fluttering banner with the Roman X over it [figure 33], and a feature of the other numbered cards is their embellishment with sketches of small groups of animals or people. In the earliest packs hearts and bells are painted red, the right half of the heart being shaded, and the

24 An engraving by Israhel von Mechenen (fifteenth-century).

25 Four nineteenth-century Swiss cards
illustrating the use of banners for aces and showing
der Ober and *der Unter*.

26 *(opposite)* Two cards from a copy of an
extremely rare, early sixteenth-century pack by
Peter Flötner.

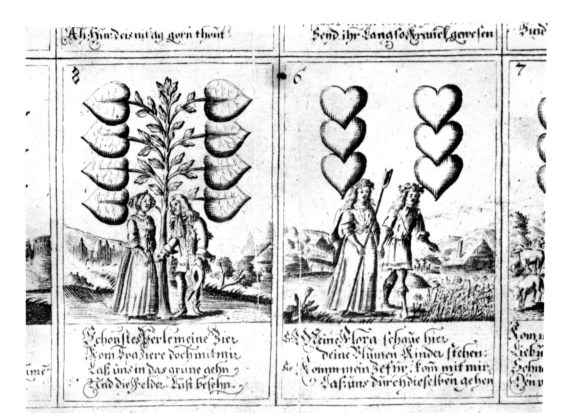

34

leaves and acorns green; later the bells became yellow and red and the acorns yellow, red and green. It is noteworthy that this colouring was never more than an ancilliary means of identification, and never became the principal, let alone the only, recognition mark.

But the German card-makers of this period did not stick rigidly to their national symbols, or, indeed, to any particular sequence. Unlike their successors, who were in all probability commercially more successful, they refused to be hampered or restricted by the cramping hand of monotonous and repetitive convention. Indulging their fancy, they varied the signs according to every capricious notion. They set no bounds to their inventiveness. Unicorns and dogs, rabbits and apes, monkeys and lions, parrots and peacocks, stroll or fly or flutter through the cardboard world [figure 30]. Packs appeared with suits of pinks, of columbines, printers' inkpads, vases, drinking-cups, books, combs, fishes, crowns, bellows, frying-pans, shields, alms-houses and knives. There were other and more freakish designs. Some cards were circular. But since they were not very practical for gambling none enjoyed more than an

28 Three cards from a Polish pack composed like a German pack but with Italian suit-marks.

27 *(opposite)* Four cards from an uncut printed sheet showing the German suit-marks of *grün* or *laub* (leaves), *herzen* (hearts), *eicheln* (acorns) and *schellen* (bells), *das Daus,* which replaced the ace as the highest card, *der Ober* which took the place of the queen, and typical sketches.

35

ephemeral popularity. A seven instead of a nine might easily be thrown upon the table, or admiration of a design might draw, momentarily but nonetheless disastrously, a player's attention from the game. Modern variations from the standard have suffered the same fate.

Nevertheless German manufacturers quickly obtained a predominant position in the playing card trade, with a vast foreign business, even challenging the inventors in their home markets. They exported great quantities of cards to Italy, Bohemia, Poland, Austria and Scandinavia. In 1441 the Signoria of Venice prohibited the importation of printed pictures and cards (the earliest record of printed cards); and a manuscript chronicle of the city of Ulm (1474) states: 'Playing cards were sent in small casks into Italy, Sicily and also over the sea, and bartered for spices and other wares.' This tremendous output, accompanied and stimulated by a fall in price, could never have been accomplished without some mechanical means of production. The ingeniously designed, exquisitely finished and surely very expensive cards of the fifteenth century could not have become the property of the general public. Before cards could find their way from the rich man's palace to the poor man's cottage, from the knight's pavilion to the soldier's tent, there had to be some method of quantity production. This was rendered possible first by the woodcutter's and then the engraver's art.

Woodblocks, said to have been invented in ancient China, were first used for printing recurrent designs on textiles. When paper became plentiful, a change in medium must readily have sprung to mind and was easily accomplished. Paper on walls would be an obvious transitional use. Undoubtedly the extended use of the innovation was provoked and accelerated by two social phenomena of the time, the rapidly spreading habit of card-playing and the popularity of pilgrimages. The latter, much practised in the fourteenth century, when they were looked upon much as, nowadays, we regard an expedition to Blackpool or Cape Cod, received a tremendous fillip 'when Boniface IX (1389–1404) extended the granting of indulgences to other places of pilgrimage than the basilicas of Rome. Cologne and Munich were the first places to receive this privilege. Such grants were confirmed by succeeding Popes, and a great influx of pilgrims to the favoured sanctuaries ensued.' (Campbell Dodgson). Religious woodcuts were distributed to the pilgrims, and the rise in numbers of the one induced a corresponding increase in the other. The ever-expanding demand for holy pictures and playing cards proceeded simultaneously, urging first the woodcutters, then the wood-engravers and then the copper-engravers and, of course, the printers to ever greater efforts. From a single shop issued indulgences, images of saints,

29 *(opposite)* Four cards from an eighteenth-century Bavarian pack printed by Andreas Benedictus Gobl, a prolific card-maker of Munich.

37

prints of Biblical scenes, the admirable *Biblia Pauperum*, with leaves printed on one side only with scenes of Christ's passion, and the Devil's pasteboards. Thus Ysenhut, a printer of Basle, called himself now *Buchdrucker* (book printer), now *Heiligendrucker* (printer of holy pictures), now *Briefmaler* (illustrator) and now *Kartenmaler* (card painter). Moreover, improvements in the technique of reproduction in quantity were accelerated by the Black Death, which swept and reswept through Europe and vastly increased the demand for the *Ars Moriendi*. This devotional manual, with its vivid pictures of horrid demons tempting a dying man to unbelief, despair and other damnations, was thrust into moribund hands as a graphic aid to the voice of the minister droning beside the deathbed and urging repentance,

30 *(above and opposite)* Eight cards from a very scarce pack engraved by Virgil Solis (1514–62). The queen and 8 of lions; the ace and king of peacocks; the knave and 6 of monkeys; the queen and 10 of parrots.

38

patience and resistance. When the rate of death became so high that an overworked priesthood could not attend all the dying, the *Ars Moriendi* enabled the patient to cope with death without professional assistance.

Whilst the de luxe cards were engraved in copper, wood-engraving was the usual method of production *en masse*. The colouring was either done by hand or stencilled, the all-inclusive sweep of the stencil brush giving rise to the German saying; '*Alle zwölf Apostel auf einen Streich machen*' – to paint all twelve Apostles at one stroke.

During the late fifteenth and early sixteenth centuries, Germany produced some exceptionally beautiful and artistic playing cards, equalling, if not surpassing, the hand-painted

cards of the Italian Renaissance which, as we have already seen, were themselves the work of miniature painters and decorative artists of the highest ability.

Among the great German engravers of the period who occasionally undertook the production of cards were the Master of the Playing Cards with sixty-six playing cards (c. 1450) and forty-four other engravings to his credit; the Master of 1466 or the monogram E.S., responsible for at least two packs and more than 300 engravings, with whose work commences a positive history of copperplate engraving in the Netherlands and Germany and from whose copper engravings the very powerful woodcuts of the *Ars Moriendi* are thought to have been derived; the Masters P.W. and F.C.Z; Virgil Solis, whose

31 Four cards showing the Swiss suits of shields, roses, bells and acorns (sixteenth-century).

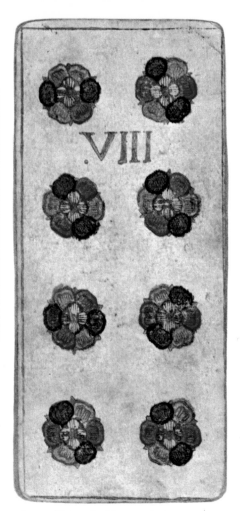

cards are, perhaps, the most beautiful of all; Israhel von Mechenen, Erhard Schoen and H.S. Beham. In addition, the designs on some cards were taken from the work of the great Martin Schongauer, Hübsch Martin, even if he did not engrave them himself.

Max Lehrs, in his monograph *Playing Cards of the Master E.S. of 1466*, published in 1892, notes:

Finally there is in the University Library of Erlangen a Bible bound in cut leather, on the cover of which we find figures and animals derived from the four of men and the three of birds; and in the Germanisches Museum a stamped leather binding (on a *Schwabenspiegel* M.S.) on which, besides various animals from the bird suit of the Master of the Playing Cards, and from the smaller set of the Master E.S., there are likewise three dogs from the seven and eight.

And the distinguished American scholars, Miss Dorothy Miner, Keeper of Manuscripts in the Walters Art Gallery, Baltimore, and Dr Hellmut Lehmann-Haupt have shown, as a result of detailed and brilliant research, that the illuminated borders of the Great Bible of Mainz, 1452–3, now in the Library of Congress,

32 Three cards from an Austrian pack of c. 1750; hand-tinted woodcuts.

41

33 Four cards of the late fifteenth century generally ascribed to Israhel von Mechenen, though sometimes attributed to Martin Schongauer. Parts of the design have certainly been taken from prints by the latter Master.

contain animals, human figures and flowers which exactly repeat down to the most minute detail figures in the cards of the Master of the Playing Cards. There are not less than nineteen such duplications, and Dr Lehmann-Haupt, in an article in the *Gutenberg-Jahrbuch* of 1962, announced his discovery of exactly similar repetitions in other Bibles, breviaries and prayer books.

Whether this correspondence means that the Master of the Bible and the Master of the Playing Cards had access to the same model book, which, judging by the animals and flowers, is thought to have belonged to a Lombardy artist, or that they were one and the same man, it clearly demonstrates that good designs and designers were then in both short supply and great demand. There is much evidence that the ever-present need of the mediaeval craftsman for patterns resulted in the better ones being copied and recopied by illuminators, engravers, leather-workers, calico-printers, wax-chandlers, gingerbread-bakers and so forth. The whole history of early engraving is bound up with the insatiable demand for choice designs.

The need for first-rate patterns presented the card-maker with a problem from which he was never entirely free. Certainly by far the largest part of his trade lay in packs with the standard sequence of bells, chalices, acorns and leaves rather than the very beautiful but highly unconventional designs of the great masters. But these he was seldom content to leave unadorned as the Italians left them. Vignettes embellished the lower part of the cards, little pictures of domestic groups or fairy tales, or drawings to show that the acorns and leaves were really growing on a tree [figure 29]. In the short run these sketches were responsible for many a charming miniature and helped to sell large quantities of playing cards; in the long run, alas, they were to prove a commercial handicap.

Fierce and, as it eventually proved, irresistible competition arose neither from Central Europe nor any country where the German sequence had become accepted, but from Switzerland where the suits were a variation on the German theme. There, acorns and bells are joined by shields replacing hearts, and flowers superseding leaves, and the aces preserve the old German banner, displaying the suit-sign on the curving fold nearest the mast [figure 25].

The gauntlet was thrown down by a pack which was so much easier to manufacture that the champion was overthrown. The new cards not only swept all before them, they hold sway to this day, leaving only pockets of territory faithful to the old symbols.

THE FRENCH AND BELGIAN PACKS

THE EARLIEST KNOWN REFERENCE to cards in France, dated 1392, is to be found in the accounts of Charles Poupart, treasurer to Charles VI. These are the pasteboards which form the basis of the oft-repeated story that playing cards were invented to cure a French king of madness. Whilst it is entirely true that Charles VI was afflicted with repeated bouts of insanity, it is only supposition that enables the work of Gringonneur to be described as playing cards. The seventeen survivors are *atouts,* and it is not known, and scarcely ever likely to be known, if Gringonneur painted the full tarot pack. It does not seem impossible that he painted only the twenty-two *atouts* which were to be used in an educational or distractive way as some form of mediaeval occupational therapy. The legend neither gives any hint as to the manner in which the cards were used nor explains why three sets were needed.

M. Poupart uses the term *'jeu de cartes'* (card-game) as if it were in common use, which in turn suggests that cards were already well-known in France. Nevertheless it is unlikely that the French had long been familiar with this invention. Only a few years earlier a most severe royal edict had been issued forbidding a wide range of sports and pastimes, while a few years later the Provost of Paris forbade card-playing, along with tennis, bowls, dice and ninepins, on work days. Since it was of the utmost importance that the citizenry, if they were ever to reach the standard set by English bowmen, should devote every moment of their spare time to practising their archery, card-playing would have been proscribed as soon as it was seen to be becoming widespread.

Whilst tarot cards, in the likeness of their Italian prototype, were manufactured and enjoyed, and for that matter still enjoy, considerable popularity in Provence, they never engaged the affections of the French. Early in the fifteenth century the latter, under the influence, it is said, of the famous knight Étienne de Vignolles, otherwise known as La Hire, fervid supporter of Jeanne d'Arc, developed the suits as we know them to-day: *coeurs, piques, carreaux* and *trèfles* (hearts, spades, diamonds and clubs) [figure 37]. The symbolic meaning of these signs is less easy to see than that of the earlier sequences; but it is suggested

34 Chardin: *The House of Cards.*

that *pique,* a lance point, stands for the aristocracy; *carreau,* an arrowhead or a paving stone, for the soldiery or citizenry; *trèfle,* a clover leaf, for fodder or peasants; and *coeur* for the Church, again, or for the courage of the soldier. From the beginning the French preferred a queen to a second knight, making the court cards king, queen and valet.

It has been fancied that these suits derive from the German because hearts occur in both, clubs have some likeness to acorns, and spades are similar to leaves. They may have been developed independently. Either way, the argument used earlier, that 'the better is the enemy of the good', supports the known documentary evidence that the French designs emerged later than the German.

The division of the four suits into two red and two black, combined with the use of pips of a very simple shape, capable of being produced by stencil, was a stroke of genius. The French treatment enormously simplified the task and cost of production and clarified the suits for the benefit of the players. From the manufacturing point of view, it is only necessary to cut the picture of one king, one queen and one knave on the block of wood or on the copper plate to get a complete pack of cards if one stencils in the suit-marks. The superiority of the French treatment, as compared with the practice in Italy, Spain or Germany, was obvious. While the German still sat over his woodblock, neatly cutting each single sign, the Frenchman had at least a hundred packs ready for distribution. The German position of dominance was gradually eroded, and by the end of the Thirty Years' War the Germans had lost their market in Scandinavia, the countries surrounding the Baltic and even some areas of Northern Germany. Everyone in those parts had become accustomed to the French suit-marks. Parts of Austria, Poland, Rumania and Hungary retained the German sequence; but from then on Germany's importance as a card-manufacturing nation steadily declined. The French challenge had resulted in victory.

Not only did France succeed Germany in her dominant position in production, but it is her design which has spread all over the world and given us cards as we know them today. The French development brought the last change in the mainstream of playing card design and began the congealment of the kings and queens and valets in curious poses and fifteenth-century clothes.

Towards the close of the sixteenth century the French manufacturers started christening the court cards with names taken from the epics of the Middle Ages, the Bible and the classics. Among them we find King David, Judas the Maccabee, Hector, Alexander the Great, Bathsheba, Judith, Roland, Valery and Jeanne d'Arc. The custom sprang up piecemeal and spread slowly. In some packs the court cards received a rich variety of

35 *(above and opposite)* Three cards from a pack designed by Gatteaux in 1816.

names and in some the king, queen and valet remained anonymous; finally in the seventeenth century a definite set of names became established. From time to time the names of contemporary heroes were used, such as that of Jean-Jacques Rousseau at the time of the Revolution; but they enjoyed only a fleeting popularity and the usual nomenclature soon reappeared.

The four kings are named David (spades), Alexander (clubs), Charlemagne (hearts) and Caesar (diamonds), representing the four monarchies, or empires, of the Jews, Greeks, Franks and Romans [figures 35 and 37]. Their fame was so widespread, so immense, that there can have been few people unfamiliar with their exploits.

The names of the real wives of the kings were never chosen for the cardboard court. They were called Pallas (spades), Greek goddess of war and wisdom, born from her father's head, instructress in ploughing and creator of the olive tree; Judith or Judic (hearts), probably the Apocryphal heroine who imperilled her life and chastity in the tent of Holofernes and escaped with his head; Rachel (diamonds), Jacob's wife, she of the twice seven years' service; and Argine (clubs), an anagram of Regina which some think refers to Juno Regina, chief goddess of ancient Rome, queen of the skies, and which others believe to be simply a 'spare file' for the convenient lampooning of a king's wife or mistress.

The knaves are La Hire (hearts), whose swashbuckling irreverence bore company with wit and intelligence; Ogier (spades), in actuality a Danish hero and in legend a knight who married, or rather was married by, Morgan le Fay, fairy sister of King Arthur; Hector (diamonds), on the whole thought to be Hector de Maris of the Round Table, though possibly Hector de Galard, a captain in the service of Charles v; and Lancelot (clubs) best-known knight of the Round Table.

Not only does no one know how this curious assortment of names came to be chosen for the pasteboard royalty, no one has even hazarded a guess. Likewise ignorance swirls around the origins of their postures, their clothes, their accoutrements, their accessories, excepting only that a lyre for King David is clearly apt; and Alan Wykes suggests in his book *Gambling* that the extended hand of the king of diamonds might be said to be grabbing and therefore appropriate to a monarch who earlier had ruled over the suit of coins. This idea is akin to the Highlander's traditional view of the Campbell, hand-outstretched, greedy and grasping. With each workshop free to draw the court cards as best met the taste of the Master Card-maker and his customers, a charming diversity of robe and weapon, pose and insignia, incidental embellishment and accompanying animal prevailed until the beginning of the eighteenth century, when a measure of restraint was introduced.

(following spread)
36 Knave and queen of spades from 'Florentine', published in Paris in 1955.

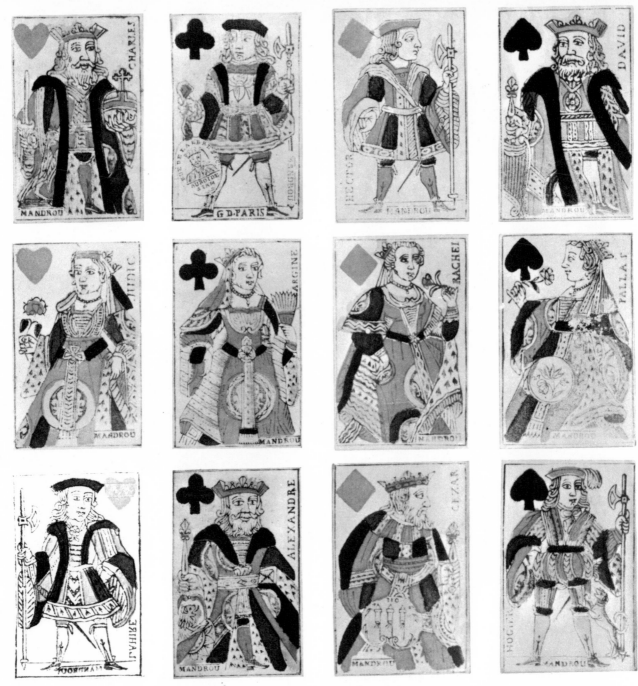

In 1701, in order to help meet the needs of the Treasury, short of funds after the long wars, the tax on cards, in abeyance for thirty years, was reintroduced. In order to hinder forgery and ease the collection of taxes, the Controller of Taxes divided the country into nine regions (mindful of the old provinces of France, the regions were Paris, Bourgogne, Lyon, Auvergne, Dauphiné, Provence, Languedoc, Guyenne and Limousin) and ordered the manufacturers of each region to use the same design

37 French court cards, each with its name, printed in Paris in about 1760.

38 Four queens from a Republican pack
(nineteenth-century).

block. If in any one region the designs varied at all, the differences were minimal and confined to the ornamentation of clothing or margins, the general appearance of the characters remaining identical with that of the official, deposited block. In 1751 the Controller imposed the Paris design on the cardmakers of Nancy, Metz, Épinal and Strasbourg. The makers of Strasbourg were said to be *dissipés et peu assidus*.

French cards were restricted to the regional designs until these were suppressed by the States General. Then, in the name of equality, one form of royalty received treatment exactly similar to the other. It was expunged, and, along with new Heads of State, a new calendar, a new era and a new (decimal) system of weights, new heads of suits came into being. *Égalité* and *Liberté*, Rousseau and Molière, Prudence and Justice, Solon and Cato were some of the new names which were possibly inspirational to the true Jacobin mind, yet scarcely likely to stir the blood of the gambler [figures 38 and 43]. In 1808 the Emperor himself took a hand in the game and had some designs of 'extreme elegance and purity' prepared for him by Gatteaux; but despite this imperial patronage they met with no better fate than other departures from the traditional figures and were withdrawn in 1813. The pre-Revolutionary royalty were restored to their courts, where they lived happily ever after.

Before we enter upon the final stage of our long journey, which has already lasted more than four hundred years, we must turn back, for a short while, almost to the starting point. It is Belgium which claims our attention. The Belgians exported

39 (left) Two triumphs from a Flemish pack illustrating the change from the traditional designs to meaningless animal scenes (c. 1810).

40 (right) Knave and queen of hearts from a Belgian pack printed in Liège (c. 1810).

massive quantities of cards to England, where the road leads next and where the main part of our story ends.

Thanks to the researches of M. Alexandre Pinchart, *chef de section aux archives générales du Royaume, Bruxelles*, writing in 1870, the Belgian documentary evidence of card-playing is older than the French; it was he who discovered the 1379 entry in the accounts of the Dukedom of Brabant. But it has neither been possible to discover when the Belgians adopted the French pack nor to establish when they first made their own cards, characteristically about $4\frac{1}{2}$ inches high and with rather heavy, matronly queens [figure 41]. In the course of his researches, M. Pinchart found the names of two Master Card-makers in the guild registers for the year 1427. They were Michel Noël and Philippe de Bos who, as the register was not the first, may easily have had predecessors. In any case, from an early date the ranks of the Belgians were strengthened by a number of French card-makers who emigrated on account of the heavy taxation in their own country. Among the later immigrants were Jean Maillart of

54

Rouen who settled in Antwerp in the sixteenth century, Nicholas Bodet also of Rouen, who established himself in Brussels in the eighteenth century, and Pierre Paulmier, born in St Malo, who moved to Belgium to work in Bruges, also in the eighteenth century.

The first Belgian city known to have a card factory is Tournai, but sooner or later workshops appeared in most of the big towns. Antwerp, Brussels, Bruges, Liège, Ghent, Namur, Dinant, Charleroi, Ypres, Nieuport, Huy, Mons and Ostend all had factories which flourished, particularly in the eighteenth century when French production was hampered by the exactions of the tax collector. In a report to the Empress Maria Theresa in 1766 it is stated that the Brussels factory, the oldest extant at the time, was staffed by thirteen Masters who had eighty-six workers in their employ. This factory exported about fifty thousand dozen packs to Holland every year. It also exported to St Petersburg and to France, though in the latter case the trade was clandestine.

42 Three cards from costume packs printed in
Paris.

CINQ-MARS.

DAME DE MONSOREAU.

In the fifteenth century the Belgian card-masters exported whole barrels of cards to England – as, indeed, they did to Germany – and continued to do so long after the English manufacture had been set up. But Belgium did not enjoy this trade without competition, the fiercest rivalry being offered by the card-makers of Rouen. Long enjoying a continuous commercial connection with Great Britain, Rouen was an important centre of the printing trade at the turn of the fifteenth and sixteenth centuries, producing a large number of liturgical books for the English market, and the home of a school of illuminators which received much encouragement from Cardinal d'Amboise (Dr A.A. Tilley, *Mediaeval France)*.

In the circumstances it is not surprising that English card-players have always used French cards or cards of French, or basically French, design. But the English card-makers, late in the field, made some changes in design, partly through muddle-headedness and partly as an assertion of their independence.

An interesting sidelight on this commerce is introduced by a remark of M. d'Allemagne in *Les Cartes à jouer du XIVe au XXe Siècle: 'Le commerce des cartes à jouer à Rouen était fort considérable avec les pays étrangers, et bien souvent les cartiers rouennais substituaient à leurs noms et enseignes les noms et marques de leurs clients.'* The names of the Belgian makers were as seldom printed on the cards they exported to England as were the French, since the London merchants, who also had a considerable re-export trade, preferred their own names to appear. As a rule, however, the manufacturer's mark was stamped on the packs: for this maker a red pig, for that a wild bear, and for yet a third a rose. The cards were shipped through the ports of l'Écluse, Flushing, Arnemuiden and Amsterdam, and the surrounding circumstances suggest that a good proportion were smuggled into Great Britain.

43 Knave of diamonds from a Republican pack, in pen-and-ink and watercolours and ascribed to David (1809–10).

THE ENGLISH PACK

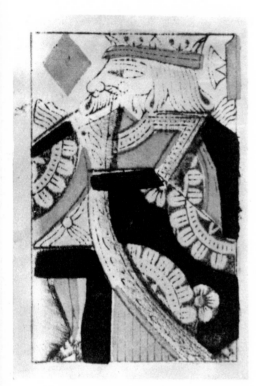

SOME TIME AFTER THE YEAR 1400, on the negative evidence that Chaucer does not mention them, and before 1463, on the positive evidence of a statute issued by Edward IV, playing cards came to England. The first packs may have been brought home by a 'soldier from the wars returning'; more likely they were in the sample bag of a Rouennais merchant, who, after discussing with his English customer a sample of fine Burgundy wine, for which Rouen was the main outlet, and drawing attention to the great beauty of a magnificent, illuminated Missal, brought out a sample of the latest continental pastime. Whatever the truth of the matter, before the end of the century cards were a common Christmas game, as is evident from the Paston Letters, that invaluable record of social and domestic customs of the fifteenth century, and were also in demand at Court. The Hon. Daines Barrington, to whom the Rev. Gilbert White addressed so many of his letters on the natural history of Selborne, reported in an article entitled 'Some Observations on the Antiquity of Card-playing in England' (*Archaeologia*, vol. VIII, 1787) that he had traced in the privy purse accounts of Henry VII three several entries of money paid out to meet card losses.

The English, very naturally, translated the names of the suits into their own language, and in doing so left for posterity more than one enigma. Why, for instance, did they base two suit names on the Italo-Spanish pack, 'spades' and 'clubs' for *spade* (plural of *spada*) and *bastoni*, rather than follow the French system throughout? Why choose the word 'diamond' for *carreau* when the contemporary word for that shape was 'lozenge'? Unfortunately no English card of an earlier date than 1675 has survived, so there is no means of knowing when, let alone why, card-names were abandoned.

On the other hand, ten court cards (with the knave of hearts and diamonds missing), produced at Rouen by Pierre Maréchal about 1675, have survived, and there is a striking resemblance between them and the full-length cards published in England up to about 1850, and even the double-ended cards of today.

In the Rouen pack all four kings are left-handed, the red kings being armed with battle-axes and the black with swords. This is faithfully repeated in the English pack, except that the king of hearts is flourishing a sword behind his head. All four kings have long hair resting on their shoulders, in the Rouen cards sadly

44　King of diamonds by J. Reynolds (1815).

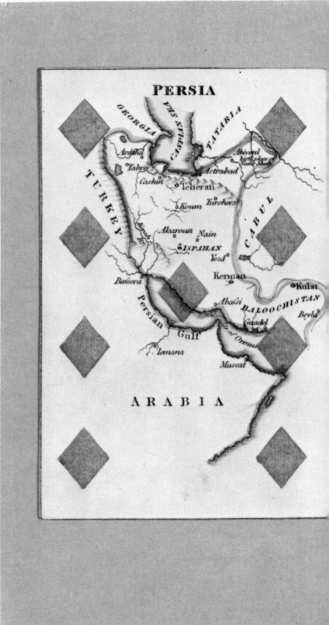

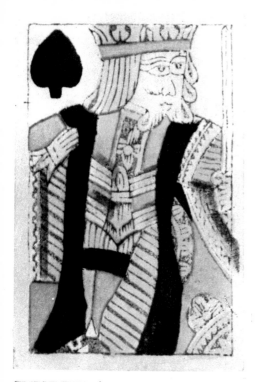

lacking the attention of a barber, but in the English portraits neatly curled upwards, inwards in the case of the red kings and outwards in the case of the black. The Rouen kings have indistinct moustaches and unkempt, forked beards; these are tidily dressed in the English version where the king of hearts is clean-shaven. All have crowns and long flowing robes with wide sleeves, the king of hearts alone enjoying a wealth of ermine trimming; the king of diamonds is in profile; and the king of clubs grasps the orb, ensign of terrestrial power under the sovereignty of Heaven. In the English pack [figures 48 and 52] the king of clubs' right hand has vanished, leaving the orb floating in mid-air.

In both packs all the queens hold a flower in their left hand and the queen of spades a sceptre in her right. In the Rouen pack the ensign of royalty has an ornate head atop a narrow shaft and more nearly resembles a mace. Each queen has Tudor lappets hanging loosely at the side of her head, and each wears a crown at the back of her head in the Elizabethan style.

The two Rouen knaves, spades and clubs, wear caps of red velvet (that of the knave of spades being scalloped), have long hair and are clean-shaven. The scalloping disappears in the early English portrait, but reappears later on in all the caps, red and black, in a form of battlementing. The Rouen knave of spades grasps a pike, his hand thrust through a billowing sleeve, whilst his English counterpart, who has a prolific moustache, holds a weapon with a queer and harmless looking head which, in fact, is no more than a grossly distorted pike-head. The knave of clubs, who in the Rouen pack was a great swaggerer, holding an arrow with a barley-sugar shaft and quite as tall as himself, becomes in the English version the most diminished of jacks. The feathers have gone from his arrow, leaving but a bald, pointed, meaningless shaft. The feather which in the early English pack jutted jauntily from his cap has now become a sad down-hanging leaf; and he, if truth be told, is now nearer a jack-straw than a jack of clubs. The English knave of hearts has also suffered badly at the hands of the artists. His right hand, which originally grasped an authoritative truncheon, now holds a frivolous feather. The truncheon's lower end slowly disappeared until only the top, looking rather like an arum lily, was left in his hand, and that, by an artist's mistake in the 1820s, was converted into a feather. Equally the knave of diamonds is unusually armed for he appears on many cards to wield a Welsh hook, or glaive, a weapon akin to a pole-axe.

English cards were no better regarded by authority than their European relations, being similarly subjected to disapproval and taxation. In 1526 Henry VIII tried, in vain, to stamp out their use; and in 1541 a statute, with some preambulatory remarks about the shocking effect of card-playing on morals, religion and

46 King of spades by Josiah Stone (c. 1815).

47 King of hearts by Hunt and Sons (1815).

45 *(opposite)* King of hearts and 9 of diamonds from the *New Geographical Cards* published by Charles Hodges in 1827.

domestic happiness, enacted that husbandmen, serving-men, labourers and the like might play cards at Christmastide only, and at no other time. Archery, of course, was the main consideration in the mind of the king, who adopted extraordinary means for encouraging the use, and supply, of the long bow. Nevertheless, and true to continental form, playing cards refused to be suppressed, and by the middle of the next reign they were used, together with dice and backgammon, for gambling and recreation throughout the country. A short time later, James I was actually putting in a good word for them:

As for sitting, or human pastimes – since they may at times supply the room which, being empty, would be patent to pernicious idleness – I will not, therefore, agree with the curiosity of some learned men of our age in forbidding cards, dice and such like games of hazard; when it is foul and stormy weather, then I say, may ye lawfully play at cards or tables; for, as to dicing, I think it becometh best deboshed soldiers to play at on the heads of their drums, being only ruled by hazard, and subject to knavish cogging; and as for chess, I think it over-fond because it is over-wise and philosophic a folly.

As Professor Kendall remarks, 'James, apparently, was not very good at chess but his balanced broadmindedness in a Puritan age commands respect.'

The taxes imposed upon playing cards, the duties levied on them, the monopolies for trading in them, and the prohibited import of them constitute in themselves a field of enquiry full of curiosity, interest and charm. It would be fascinating to speculate at length on the costume, duties and rewards of the sixteenth- and seventeenth-century Inspectors of Playing Cards, one of whom, Sir Richard Coningsby, Kt, in return for a rent of £200 per annum enjoyed the sole right to collect a levy of five shillings a gross of packs. This monopoly was granted by James I 'in recompense of £1,800 due to him from the king, and of his patent for the sole export of Tin granted by the late queen'. There appears to be no evidence as to whether Sir Richard showed a profit, suffered a loss or broke even on the deal; but from the king's point of view it seems a singularly cheap way of discharging a debt. Sir Walter Raleigh was another monopolist, though for so short a time that he could have gained little from the privilege.

In 1628 there occurred an event of twofold significance, the foundation of the Worshipful Company of Makers of Playing Cards by charter dated 22 October of that year. This long and wordy document, after drawing harrowing attention to the inability of the card-makers of London 'to maintain themselves their wives and their families thereby, partly by means of the many deceits and abuses by such as are inexpert in that trade... but principally by reason of the continued importing of great quantities of Foreign Playing Cards made in the parts beyond the

48 *(opposite)* Six court cards from a pack printed by I. Hardy.

63

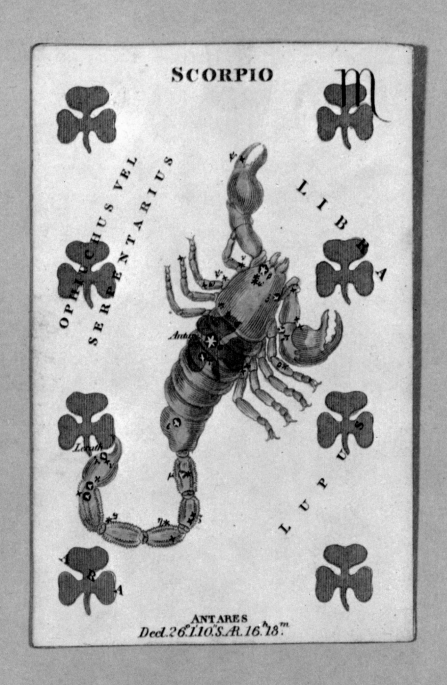

seas' most carefully points out 'that the Customs' impositions and other duties upon Foreign playing Cards heretofore wont to be imported and brought into this realm' had been substantial. The Charter proceeds to forbid, absolutely, the importation of cards from overseas, which are to be forfeited and confiscated; constitutes the Company in the name of 'The Master, Wardens and Commonalty of the Mistery of Makers of Playing cards of the City of London', and only then, after so many decent preliminaries, reaches its true significance in the royal mind. 'As a competent recompense', to the king and his successors, 'for the loss and diminution which we or they may have in our Customs' impositions and other duties upon Foreign playing Cards,' the Company agrees to pay a duty of two shillings per gross packs on all playing cards and a further one shilling per gross packs to the officer appointed as Receiver of the Duty. And to ensure that the revenue shall suffer as little diminution as possible the Company further agrees to make sufficient playing cards to supply the kingdom 'at as cheap and low rates and prices as Foreign Cards have been sold in England during the past seven years'.

Despite protestations by the House of Commons, notably in 1631, against taxes levied without its consent, and petitions by the Worshipful Company asserting that they still could not support their families by reason of the heavy taxes, which they appear to have found as crippling as foreign competition, the taxation of cards had come to stay for more than three hundred years. We who live in the twentieth century know well the extreme reluctance with which any Government abandons a source of revenue. In 1710 Parliament, amongst other new duties designed to raise 'a Yearly Fond of One hundred eighty-six thousand six hundred and seventy pounds ... for carrying on the War and other Her Majesties occasions,' enacted 'that from and after the Eleventh Day of June One thousand seven hundred and eleven, during the Term of Thirty Two Years from thence next ensuing, there shall be Raised, Levied, Collected and Paid' a tax of 6d per pack, which was increased to 1s per pack in 1756, 1s 6d in 1776, 2s in 1789 and 2s 6d in 1804, this last again to help pay for England's wars. This high duty led to evasion of payment and the tax was reduced to 1s in 1828, when an annual licence of 5s was imposed, against a penalty of £100 and forfeiture of material and execution of a bond in the 'penal sum of £500', and finally to 3d per pack in 1862, at which level it remained until the abolition of the duty in 1960.

The act of 1710 laid down that cards were not to be removed from the 'House or place of Making' until 'a seal upon the Paper and Thread inclosing every Pack of Cards shall be put thereupon as the Commissioners for the said Duties on Stampt Vellum, Parchment and Paper, shall from time to time devise and appoint'. In the following year a second act, amending the

49 (opposite) 8 of clubs from an astronomical pack published by Charles Hodges (c. 1830).

THOMAS CRESWICK

earlier, required that 'one of the Cards of each pack or Parcel… shall be also Marked or Stamped on the Spotted or Painted side thereof'. One wonders by what caprice the Commissioners for the Stamp Duties chose the ace of spades as the card to be stamped; but choose it they did, and from that year on it became the duty card, its unofficial position being fully legalized in the law of 1765 [figure 50].

When the duty was raised to 1s 6d in 1776, that is to say 6d more than the 6d inherent in the ace of spades plus the 6d stamped on the wrapper, the words SIXPENCE ADD DUTY were printed on the ace, the first word being to the left of the card and the last two to the right. When the tax was raised to 2s the same words were repeated above the ace; and when increased to 2s 6d the words TWO SHILLINGS were printed to the left and AND SIXPENCE to the right. In 1828, when the tax was reduced to 1s, a new and ornate ace, with the spade sign encircled by intricate lathe work and supported by the lion and the unicorn, was introduced by the Commissioners, who contracted the work of printing to Messrs Perkins Bacon & Co., noted printers of bank notes and, later, postage stamps. It became known familiarly, and quite understandably, as 'Old Frizzle'. Instead of reverting to the original practice of letting the ace and wrapper speak for themselves the words DUTY ONE SHILLING were printed over the top of the design. This act also provides that: 'No cards … are to be made in any Places in Great Britain but London, Westminster or Southwark.'

After being printed with twenty aces each, from engraved plates paid for by the manufacturers, the sheets were returned by the Commissioners and pasted on normal pasteboard in the same way as any other top sheet. The boards were then cut and the aces used as required. To conclude the process, an Excise officer called at intervals and affixed 'a Label, in such Manner, and with such Mark or Device thereon, as the said Commissioners shall direct'. Accounts were than to be delivered monthly, verified on oath, and settled ten days later. This system lasted until 1862, when approved manufacturers were licensed to sell playing cards and to print their own aces of spades, the duty being denoted on the wrapper which was required so long as playing cards were taxed. Through all its variations in design and value the ace of spades was, and is, the only copyright card in the pack.

The second function of the Worshipful Company was super-vision of the trade in the City of London and throughout its suburbs and liberties 'and all other towns and parishes and places within Ten miles any way from the said City'. To enable it to do so the Charter provided that only a Freeman or someone who had served a seven years' apprenticeship was allowed to set up or exercise 'The Art, Trade or mistery of making of playing

50 *(above and opposite)* Four aces of spades showing different rates of tax. 'Old Frizzle' appears top right. The lower ace was used after the legal requirement for a 'duty card' had ceased.

cards'; and that all cards were to be sealed by a Receiver, who must always be a Freeman, and that every maker was to register 'a print, stamp or mark of his own name or invention' so that the Receiver could identify the makers of the cards brought before him.

An extraordinary number and variety of marks were registered, since it was by no means necessary for a manufacturer to confine himself to a single mark. For example, on 22 August 1654, Master Robert Browne registered The Bacchus, The Cupid, The Edward I Shilling and The Maidenhead. Royalist marks included The Royal Oak and The King's Head, and among later Royal marks were Princess Anne of Denmark, The Orange Tree, The Tulipp and Crowne, and Queen Anne. Among inn signs used as marks were The Lurking Lion, The Austridge, The Three Nags Head, the Cocke and Hoope, the Harty Choake and The Sleeping Man.

In April 1741 Mr Blanchard, one of the larger manufacturers, registered The Great Mogul, and in October of the following year complained of an infringement of his rights by a certain Thomas Hill, who was neither a Freeman nor in any way connected with the Worshipful Company. Mr Hill was entirely unimpressed by the protests made to him, and now that their powers were openly challenged the Company found that it was unable to protect its Freemen, and in consequence its authority declined. In the next century the marks seem to have become more or less common property, and four at least were used throughout the trade to denote the grades into which packs were sorted. The top quality was indicated by The Great Mogul; the second by Henry VIII; the third by The Valiant Highlander; and the fourth by The Merry Andrew.

In 1882, at the annual banquet to mark the inauguration of the new Master and Wardens, each Liveryman – a grant of livery had been applied for and granted in 1792 – was given a pack of cards specially designed for the occasion, since when a similar gift has been made every year. A portrait of the Master for the year is shown in the centre of the ace of spades, with his name and those of the two Wardens and the Clerk printed below; on the back is a design illustrating an important event of the year [figure 63]. Thus the series of packs makes an interesting historical record.

The last chapter in the story of the development of the true four-suited pack has now been reached. It opens with Thomas de la Rue, a Guernseyman living in London, being granted Royal Letters Patent on 3 February 1832 for the printing of cards by letterpress and lithography. Greatly improved output enabled him to reduce prices with the result that sales increased. The tax reduction in 1862 stimulated consumption throughout the

country, and the 296,660 packs sealed in 1861 increased to 732,960 in 1864. With mass production, falling prices and tax reduction, small workshops were swallowed up by larger, Master Card-makers found work as employees, and cards became standardized. To add insult to injury, the very expressions of the cardboard court have been crystallized in commercialism. The kings' looks have become those of company directors, strained and indicative of ulcers, while the queens and knaves have taken on the airs of the attendant secretaries: the personal are pawky, and the company ones circumspect. Efforts have been made, from time to time, to introduce entirely new designs; but since any departure from the standard means a high price, and as serious card-players are, and always have been, extremely reluctant to accept any change, no innovation has ever met with more than a limited success. Thomas de la Rue was without doubt a very great printer; yet that very genius proved calamitous to this small branch of the graphic arts. Reversing Dr Johnson's comment on Dryden's effect on literature, it might be said of Thomas de la Rue that he found a small quantity of marble and left a great quantity of brick.

Apart from the additions of intricate patterns or small pictures on the back, often designed by eminent artists and with the commercial merit of masking faults in the paper and thereby enabling a cheaper grade to be used, the most important modern improvements accepted by players are the change from single to double-ended court cards and the addition of indices. These became standard about 1865–70 (although double-ended cards can be found as far back as the seventeenth century). The first were devised to avoid revealing to an opponent, when 'sorting' a hand, the presence of court cards, and the latter, an American idea, were called into being by the tightly held poker hand, fanned out only just sufficiently to enable the player to identify a card. If we include the modern 'pneumatic finish', invented by William Thomas Shaw, a partner in Thomas de la Rue & Co., in the last quarter of the century, which enables one card to slide easily over another and the pack to be easily shuffled and dealt, a decrease in size and the addition of the joker (another American notion) we have noted all the major alterations in playing cards in the last one hundred and fifty years or so.

51 *(opposite)* Court cards from a pack printed by Thomas de la Rue in 1832, in which year he was granted Royal Letters Patent for his system of printing playing cards in colour.

52 *(above and opposite)* Four kings by
Hall & Son (*c.* 1815).

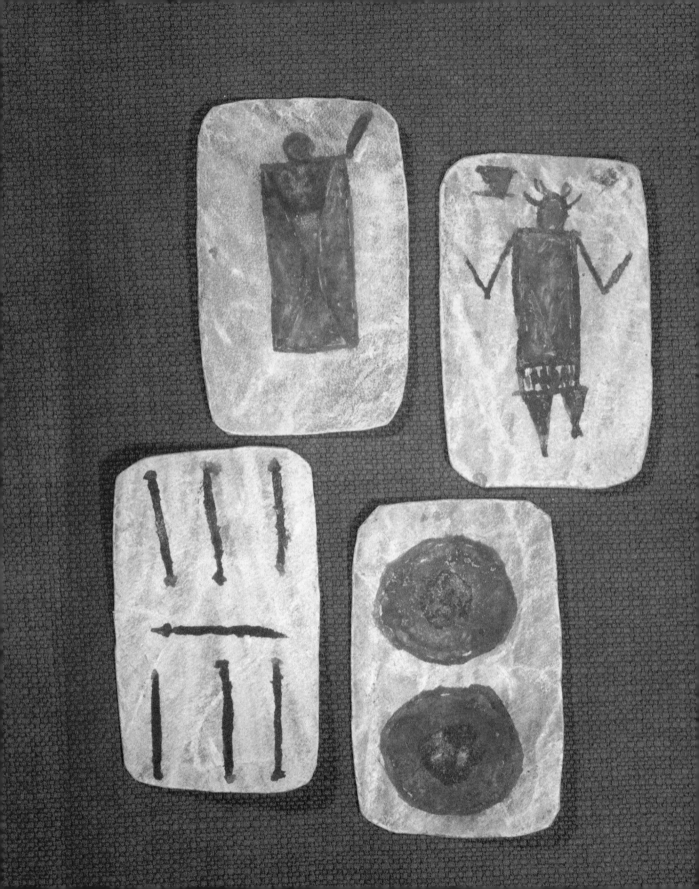

THE AMERICAN AND RUSSIAN PACKS

How did the English pack reach North America? Cards seem unlikely baggage for either the Pilgrim Fathers or subsequent waves of Puritans, yet Catherine Perry Hargrave has traced a Plymouth County record, dated 1633, of several persons being fined £2 each for card-playing. Was this the work of an apostate Puritan, or were cards introduced into God-fearing, nonconformist Plymouth by a dissolute Dutchman from Nieuw Amsterdam or some graceless Englishman from Jamestown? It is, perhaps, of little importance; what is of consequence is that this design rather than the Spanish, introduced by Columbus and Cortes more than a hundred years earlier, gained general acceptance throughout the continent.

America was relatively late in starting the manufacture of playing cards, long relying on imports from England. The first native card-maker, so far as is known, was Jazaniah Ford of Milton, Mass., who was born in 1757 and expressed his nationality by giving at least one of his kings a distinctly American cast of countenance – lantern-jawed and reminiscent of Abraham Lincoln, Jefferson Davis and Uncle Sam [figure 56]. Having shown the way, he was quickly followed by Amos Whitney (born 1766), Thomas Crehore (born 1769) and Lewis I. Cohen, each of whom established a prosperous business despite the marked preference of the general public for goods which were of English origin. This partiality was so strong that to combat it some American makers went so far as to print the word 'London', with or without the name of an imaginary English printer, on the ace of spades. An excellent example is:

Another deck, which has always been thought to be of American manufacture, and which is said to have been used by Dolly Madison at the White House, has an ace which is unique among any I have seen. It is printed in colours, red, blue, green and gold. The design resembles that of an early tax ace; a crown surmounts the garter which encircles the spade symbol. It is surrounded by a garland of green leaves which include a rose and thistle on each lower corner. Above the crown is the word 'Exportation'. On the garter are the words 'Stamp Office'. Beneath the whole design is the inscription 'Jones & Co. London'. What are we to make of this?

(So wrote Dr Allan J. Ryan of Meriden, Conn. USA, well-known card collector and historian, in private correspondence, who may well ask this question.)

The career of Lewis I. Cohen bears an astonishing resemblance to that of Thomas de la Rue. Cohen was born and, except for the

54 The seal of the Russian Government Monopoly from the ace of diamonds.

53 (opposite) Four cards from a Sioux Indian pack. Painted on skin, presumably deer hide, and obtained from an officer of the United States Army in 1869.

period 1815–19, lived all his life in the United States. The four years outside America were spent in London, where he served an apprenticeship to his half-brother, Solomon Cohen, black-lead pencil manufacturer of Houndsditch. On his return to the States, Cohen became successively a pencil manufacturer, a stationer and a playing card manufacturer. He published his first pack in 1832, invented in 1835 a machine for printing at one impression the four colours on the foreside of his cards, and retired in 1854. Thomas de la Rue was born in Guernsey, was apprenticed to a printer in that island, emigrated to London and became successively a straw hat manufacturer, a manufacturing stationer and a playing card manufacturer, published his first pack in 1832, received in that year Royal Letters Patent for his method of printing cards, and retired on 31 December 1858.

Moreover, it is not only the lives of the two men which are alike; so also are their cards. Catherine Perry Hargrave says of the Cohen cards: 'they are much like the English ones of the period... They have typical English wrappers... Owen Jones designs for their card-backs, the fact being mentioned both on the wrappers and the aces of spades.' Indeed one of the later aces of spades is an exact reproduction, with the exception of the

55 Four cards from a pack by J. Y. Humphries of Philadelphia (c. 1800). In this finely engraved, hand-coloured pack the diamonds are red, the hearts lake, the spades blue and the clubs green. The kings are eminent Americans, the queens classical goddesses and the knaves chiefs of various Indian tribes. The king of hearts is a reproduction of Gilbert Stuart's second, Lansdowne-type portrait of George Washington, and the queen of diamonds is Fortune with her wheel, indicative of a fickle nature.

lettering, of the ace introduced by Thomas de la Rue & Co. in 1862 when the change in the law allowed card-makers to print their own. The association between Thomas de la Rue & Co. and Owen Jones, prominent English architect, decorator and lithographer, who was responsible for the interior decoration of the buildings for the Great Exhibition of 1851, was well known. The backs of many De la Rue cards were to his designs. The conclusion that there was some connection between Lewis I. Cohen and Thomas de la Rue, or at least between their firms, is irresistible. What that connection was has yet to be discovered.

After his retirement in 1854, Cohen's business was carried on by his son Solomon and his nephew John M. Lawrence, under the style of Lawrence and Cohen, until 1871, when it was converted into a public company, the New York Consolidated Card Company. This company introduced corner indices to the English pack, presumably deriving the idea from early nine-teenth-century Spanish cards on which an index can sometimes be seen in the top right-hand corner. Indexed cards, one of the very few accepted changes in card design in the last hundred years or so, were first known as 'squeezers'. They were quickly challenged by the products of another New York firm, Andrew Dougherty and Company, who offered strong opposition by producing packs with miniature card faces in the upper left-hand corners and called, from their three faces, 'triplicates'. After a period of intense competition between the two companies, according to Catherine Perry Hargrave, 'a tacit understanding about sales territory was commemorated in a card-back of 1877, showing two bulldogs straining at their leashes in front of their respective houses. On the collar of one is "Squeezer"; on the other "Trip".' Both were imported into England, with fine impartiality, by Mudie & Sons, proprietors of the celebrated Victorian circulating library.

There were, of course, other American card-makers, such as J. Y. Humphries, of Philadelphia, who produced some charm-ingly engraved packs at the beginning of the nineteenth century, Samuel Hart and Company, also of Philadelphia, in the middle, and Russell and Morgan of Cincinnati, later to become the mighty United States Playing Card Company, publishers of the well-known Bicycle Brand cards, towards the end. Their packs were well produced, and mostly they gave their kings and queens and knaves happy expressions, often with smiles, in con-tradistinction to the frowns of their English cousins.

As we have seen, America must also be credited with another innovation: the joker. At first this was known as the 'best bower', a name derived from the game of euchre, a modified form of écarté, in which the knave of the suit of trumps is called the right bower, and is the highest trump, and the other knave of the same colour is called the left bower, and is the second

56 King of clubs from a faro pack by Samuel Hart (c. 1850), apparently printed from the late eighteenth-century blocks of Jazaniah Ford.

highest trump. The best bower was of greater value than any other card.

While the restless American temperament, apt to innovation, has led that people to print many special purpose packs, commemorative, advertising and souvenir packs, humorous and fanciful designs, dice packs and chess packs, to pioneer the use of colour photography for the foresides and to produce back designs in great variety and beauty, no other alterations to the English pack have gained acceptance. It seems unlikely that they ever will, and likely that the cardboard head that wears a crown can sleep easily at night.

If Thomas de la Rue's influence on American playing cards was inconsiderable, indirect and indistinct, his effect on Russian cards was direct, notable and plain. An article in Chambers' Journal for July 1846 makes the position clear:

At one time Russia was one of the best customers in Europe for playing cards; but this trade is now at an end, in consequence of that country having engaged in the manufacture itself; nor, judging from the quantity it makes away with does this seem unreasonable. In Russia card-playing is a universal amusement, and will in all probability continue to be so while the people remain illiterate, and political speculation is attended with danger. To supply the demand for cards, the government took the fabrication of the article into its own hands, and with much liberality not only purchased from Mr de la Rue a knowledge of the manufacture but induced his brother to take entire charge of the establishment in which the cards are made. The quantity of cards thus made annually for Russian consumption is a million of packs, the profits on the sale of which are devoted to charity.

Paul de la Rue, who is listed in the London Street Directories for the years 1830–39 as a maker of straw hats, with premises in Lambs Conduit Street, became, almost overnight, the largest card manufacturer in the world at that time, and one of the largest of any time. It was not until 1873 that the production of all the English manufacturers together passed the million mark, whilst in the meantime Russian output had streaked ahead. W. A. Chatto, a most cautious author, writes in *Facts and Speculations on the History and Origin of Playing Cards* (1848): 'Though 14,400 packs were manufactured daily yet the supply was unequal to the demand and a petition had been presented to the Emperor for a more liberal supply.' This daily figure indicates an annual production of the order of 4,000,000, an immense output in itself even if the more liberal supply was not granted. The profits of this vast enterprise went towards the upkeep of the great Foundling Hospitals in Moscow and St Petersburg, founded by Catherine the Great, though it is legitimate to speculate on the percentage retained by the officer of public charity who administered the hospitals.

Neither quantity nor monopoly were in this case the enemies

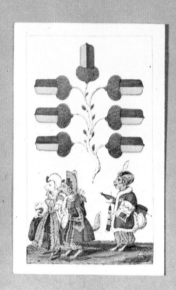

of quality, for Russian packs were of the highest standard both in printing and materials. The French suit-signs (the Monopoly printed cards with German symbols as well as French until well into the nineteenth century) have an individual character, the tips of the spades and hearts and the stem of the clubs being unusually prolonged. Sometimes the cards are embellished with animated scenes incorporating Cossacks or Chinamen or other whimsical figures. Always, however, the seal of the Monopoly appears at least once. This seal, more often than not printed in gold, was a pelican 'in her piety' over an inscription in Russian signifying 'For the benefit of the Foundling Hospital' [figure 54].

Despite the very high standard of production and the skill of her designers, Russia added nothing to the history of playing cards themselves, though she made a unique contribution to card-games. For instance, biritsch, a Russian version of whist, reached England in 1894 and became 'bridge' (a corruption of the original name).

58 Four nineteenth-century Russian cards from a pack printed with German suit-signs.

57 *(opposite)* Three court cards from a pack printed in about 1890.

60 Queen of spades from a German copy of the
Jeu des Reynes Renomées.

59 *(opposite)* Four cards from a Russian pack
satirizing religion (*c.* 1930).

PLAYING CARDS, as remarked in the very first sentence of this book, have had many uses in addition to gaming, the most frequent being some sort of instruction. Leaving aside the Tarot whose nature is, in any case, not firmly established, cards intended for the furtherance of education usually have the symbols confined to one end, or one corner, of the foreside and the resultant space is filled with the information to be absorbed, more or less unconsciously, by the student. Occasionally suit-signs and memoranda are intermingled. In the course of play with these cards the scholar supposes himself to be merely playing a game, but is in truth acquiring, by a sort of cerebral osmosis, the lessons printed on the cards. In time, card lessons covering a multitude of subjects, philosophy, heraldry, history, geography, astronomy and arithmetic among them, were originated, many of the packs being splendid examples of the arts of the designer, the engraver and the printer.

The first instructive cards were contrived by a Franciscan monk of German birth, Dr Thomas Murner, scholar, poet, satirist and bitter opponent of Martin Luther. Printed in 1507 at Cracow, where Murner was then a professor of philosophy, these cards were devised in order to help the inventor's students over an intellectual stile erected by the writings of a Spanish pedant. So successful was the method that the learned Father was suspected of magic, of being hand-in-hand with the Devil. In grave danger of being burnt, he was only saved from immolation by production of the cards. When the pack was inspected by his detractors they changed their minds, much admired the cards and gave their approval to this new method of teaching. Indeed their encouragement emboldened Dr Murner to issue a second edition, printed at Strasbourg two years later, and to design another pack, published in 1518, to help inculcate the Institutes of Justinian.

Despite their successful introduction, educational cards were slow to catch on, perhaps from a lingering fear, despite the inventor's exoneration, of the fiery punishment sure to follow a successful charge of witchcraft. At all events the next such pack known, '*Das Geistliche Deutsche Cartenspil*' by Andream Strobl, was not published until 1603; it appeared at Sulzbach to a chorus of approval from high church dignitaries. Hargrave says: 'Each of the eight cards of the four suits of hearts, bells,

Coleman drawn to his execution.

Reddin standing in ye Pillory.

Pickerin Executed.

The Execution of the 5 Iesuitts.

Le marquis de Brandebourg.

Parti de deux coupé de trois traits de diverses alliances et Principautez de cette Alasse et sur le tout d'azur au Sceptre d'or en pal qui est de l'Electorat. Triple heaume et triple Cimier.

61 (above) Four cards from a 1679 pack illustrating the *Pretended Popish Plot*.

62 (below) 5 of spades from de Brianville's *Jeu de Blason*. It was first published in 1658 and there were more than a dozen editions over the next seventy or eighty years.

leaves and acorns are represented in Biblical illustrations with a decorative border, and the suit-sign unobtrusively but unfailingly shown. They are finely engraved copper plates, and there are nearly three hundred pages of text for each suit.' The huge text which, after all, was contrary to the original idea, may well have repelled the scholars and made them wary when invited to take a hand; but whatever the case, yet another forty years passed before the idea became generally accepted.

In 1643, Cardinal Mazarin, to advance the education of Louis XIV, then a child of eight, proposed a series of card games calculated to stimulate the royal mind. Jean Desmarets, a member of the Académie Française, prepared the games and in 1644 published an explanation of them under the title *Les Jeux de Cartes des Roys de France, des Reines Renommées, de la Géographie, et des Fables, cy-devant dediez à la Reine Régente, pour l'instruction du Roi*. Engraved by the noted Florentine, Stefano della Bella, the cards are of great interest to the general public, as well as the pupil, on account of both their textual and artistic merits [figures 60 and 64–66].

Since heraldry long formed an important branch of polite education, it is not surprising to find the rules of blazonry displayed on cards. In 1655 M. Claude Orence Fine, *dit de Brianville, conseiller et aumônier du Roy*, set the ball rolling with the '*Jeu d'armoiries des Souverains et états d'Europe, pour apprendre le blason*', issued at Lyons, which in the course of the next ten years ran into not less than eight editions [figure 62]; but either through naivety or a poor sense of diplomacy Fine made the mistake of exhibiting on the knaves the heraldic devices of several princely Houses. He was imprisoned, and only

regained his freedom by recalling each and every pack and replacing the low-born knave with a high-born chevalier. An heraldic pack dedicated to the Duke of Albermarle was issued in London about 1675 by Richard Blome, and one called 'Arms of the English Peers' appeared in 1684. The *'Jeu de Cartes du Blason, publié à Lyons'*, by Père F. C. Menestrier, beautifully engraved, made its appearance in 1692. The following year, the Germans, not to be outdone, printed in Nuremberg a pack showing the reigning families of Europe; in 1694 the Scots joined in with a very famous, now very scarce, pack, which was printed in Edinburgh, and was one of the few ever to be originated in Scotland. In about 1698 the *'Jeu Héraldique'* was published by Daumont in Paris. In 1719 Germany also presented an Augsburg reprint of the Daumont pack; but unfortunately, presumably because the engraved plates were an exact copy of the French originals, the designs appeared in reverse, giving a result artistically satisfactory but heraldically nonsensical.

M. Daumont, not satisfied with promoting the study of heraldry, gave much attention to another facet of knightly study, and within a short space of time issued two packs intended to teach military science, the *'Jeu de la Guerre'* [figure 68] and also the *'Jeu des Fortifications'* [figure 77]. The former is a particularly attractive pack, each card engraved with lively little scenes illustrative of a written account of some military operation; some of these pictures are alive with officers on their chargers, running soldiers and billowing smoke from the artillery. Another card gives instruction on the clearing of a battlefield after victory, and shows the dead, stripped, being bundled into a common grave – a subject seldom, if indeed ever, illustrated elsewhere.

The Swiss contributed to military knowledge by publishing in Geneva, in 1744, the 'Nouveau Jeu d'Officiers', each card of which portrays a figure in uniform taken from a series of prints variously called 'Costumes Militaires de 1740', 'Troupes irrégulières au Service de l'Autriche' and other titles (there is no fixed name for the series) by Martin Englebrecht. In this there are more than 150 figures, and even today it constitutes an important source for the study of military uniforms.

It must not be thought that the use of playing cards as a teaching aid was confined to the more exclusive or arcane sciences. Many subjects were treated in this way, many educative packs turned out; so great a multitude, indeed, that we can only touch the fringe. In 1651, for instance, 'Scientall Cards', 'written by a Lover of ingenuity and Learning', for 'acquiring without labour but with much delight and profit' the 'Rudiments of so necessary an art as Grammar' were 'sold by Baptist Pendleton, Card-maker, at his House neere St Dunstan's Church in the East'. F. Jackson MA threw his net wide by producing in 1656 'The Scholers Practicall Cards' with instructions for their use in

Elisabeth

Reyne d'Angleterre. Elle gouuerna
Sagement son Royaume, et demeura
fille jusqu'à la mort, ayant rejetté
l'alliance des plus grands Roys de
l'Europe .

habile

Jason .

Fils d'Eson Roy de Theßalie. alla
en Colchos auec les Argonautes,
et conquit la toyson d'or auec l'ayde
de Medeé, ayant endormy le dra-
gon qui la gardoit. il s'enfuit auec
elle, qui depuis estant repudiée tua
leurs enfans, et s'enfuit sur vn char
tiré par des dragons . | G. 55

56ᵉ

*regna
15 ans*

Charles huict.ᵉ

Magnanime, clement, liberal .
il conquit la Bretagne et se l'asseura
par le mariage d'Anne. il conquit
aussy le Royaume de Naples et de
Sicile; et au retour il gagna la batail-
le de fornoüe contre tous les Princes
d'Italie liguez contre luy .

N. 1.

Puckle's Machine

*A rare invention to Destroy the Crond
Of Fools at Home instead of Foes Abroad:
Fear not my Friends, this terrible Machine,
They're only Wounded that have Shares therein.*

64 *(above left)* 4 of hearts from *Jeu des Reynes
Renommées* (1644).

65 *(above centre)* Ace of diamonds from *Jeu des
Fables* (1644).

66 *(above right)* Ace of clubs from *Jeu des Rois de
France* (1644).

67 *(below)* 8 of spades from 'All the Bubbles' 1720.

spelling, writing, ciphering and casting-up accounts; and 1665
saw the beginning of a whole series of English-printed geographical cards of which we have space to mention only a part.

In the first of this sequence, printed by H. Winstanley at
Littlebury, Essex, each card has an engraving of the inhabitants
and the chief city of the foreign country with which it deals
above a textual description based, no doubt, on the latest
information available but which, nowadays, seems droll in its
inaccuracy. The eight of clubs, for example, begins 'California
most properly is a great island …'.

The second of the series, published in 1675, dealt solely with
England and in each card of the pack 'you have a map of the
county with the chiefe townes and rivers, a compass for the
bearings and a scale for mensuration, there is also given the
length, breadth and circumference of each county, the latitude of
the chief citty or towne, and its distance from London, first the
reputed, then the Measured Miles by Esquire Ogilby'. John
Ogilby, a Scot who was successively dancing-master, master-of-
revels, translator of the classics, theatre proprietor and publisher,
was ruined first by the Civil War and then by the Great Fire of
London. Re-establishing himself after the Great Fire, he printed
many fine works, concentrating in his later years on well-
illustrated geographical books, road books and atlases. He was
appointed King's Cosmographer and Geographic Printer. His
road maps were produced on narrow lengths of paper printed to
resemble ribbon. This pack [figure 75], issued by Robert

Morden and sold by him at 'The Atlas in Cornhill', is a splendid example of the engraver's and printer's arts and far superior to a pack published years later, in 1799, by J. Wallis of Ludgate Street.

The Wallis pack shows 'the geography of England and Wales accurately delineated on fifty-two cards including the boundaries, extent, products, manufactures etc. of each county' and is without the pictorial charm of the detailed maps of the earlier pack. Here the county towns alone are plotted against a rough outline filled with trees and hillocks and an occasional sheep, cow or cathedral and edged, where appropriate, with a sailing-ship or two and a large unidentifiable fish. These small pictures, masked and spoilt by the suit-sign in the centre, are surrounded by written information. Some of the notes are captivating. DARBIE-SHIRE, for instance, is 'Tillable, Rockie and Craggid'. NORTHFOLKSH's greatest Gaynes are by Herrings'; whilst of WILTSHIRE we are told: 'Wilton was once the head town but Sarisbury now is the Chief Citty. Its Cathedral was once famous, the water now runs through every streete.' The most attractive pack in the series, indeed among the finest ever printed, is one published by Charles Hodges of Portman Street in 1827 [figure 45]. Known as 'The New Geographical Cards', the aces have maps of the four continents (Australia is shown as part of Asia) and the other cards have maps of the countries comprising them. The hearts are carmine, the clubs green trefoils, the spades blue pikeheads, the court cards have in three suits full-length portraits of contemporary rulers and in the fourth a youthful George Washington as king, and Indians as queen and jack.

68 Ace, 6 and king of spades from *Jeu de la Guerre*, c. 1710. This game, first issued in 1668, was designed by Gilles de Boissière and engraved by Pierre le Pautre.

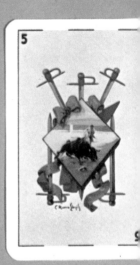

Card-makers have been as generous with their space to history as ever they were to geography. In the Cromwellian era this may have been connected with the thought that their products enabled a Puritan-dominated England to enjoy a game of cards under the guise of praiseworthy self-instruction. Louis XIV, as a boy, was required to study, as well as geography, the kings of France and the deeds of renowned queens in the cards designed by Desmarets. Young Germans of the seventeenth century pondered copies of the same cards, which were available with German texts and suit-signs, as well as a pack of Famous Personages printed in Augsburg in 1685 by Johann Strindberg. These sedate cards have at their top a bust of the Personage enclosed in a roundel with circumferential decoration, a suit-sign set amongst the decoration in the top right-hand corner, and below the hero's achievements reduced to a dozen lines of print. According to the king of clubs 'Cicero was the most famous and most excellent orator ever known to the Romans'.

The English enjoyed a splendid run of historical packs, though it must be observed that the compilers of the cards were often unashamedly partisan. As Dean Inge has pointed out, historians have been vouchsafed the power, denied to Providence, of altering the past. The tone was set in one of the earlier packs which was published on behalf of the Cavalier cause and satirizes the Rump Parliament. It was advertised as 'The knavery of the Rump, Lively represented in a pack of cards. To be sold by R.T. near Stationer's Hall...'. The four of hearts shows strips of meat being barbecued and bears the legend, 'The Rump roasted salt it well it stinks exceedingly' whilst the six of diamonds refers to the Parliamentary officer Major Kelsey as 'a sneaking bodice maker...'.

This was followed by 'All the Popish Plots, from the Armada in 1588 to the Popish Plot of 1678' (issued 1679), 'The Pretended Popish Plot' (1679) [figure 61], 'The Events of the Reign of the Queen Anne' (1710) [figure 73], 'The Impeachment of Dr Sacheverell' (from the point of view of his partisans, 1710), 'The Bubble Companies' (satirizing several remarkable 'get-rich-quick' commercial projects, 1720, and emulated by a Dutch card-maker), and in 1813 Baker & Co's 'Eclectic Cards for England, Ireland, Scotland and Wales, being a selection or an Eclectic Company of Twelve of the most eminent personages that ever distinguished themselves in their Countries for their Heroic Deeds, Wisdom,' (c. 1837). In the last pack the red suits remain unaltered, but the black suits are changed to swords and acorns, the swords being the *spata* or two-edged heavy sword. England is represented by the suit of acorns, which has a marginal decoration of oak leaves and roses, Ireland by hearts and a shamrock, Scotland diamonds and a thistle, and Wales swords and a leek. The court cards are a diverse, unusual and

71 *(above)* A card from an 1866 Scottish reproduction of a seventeenth-century pack published on behalf of the Cavalier cause.

72 *(below)* 9 of clubs from a pack of love mottos published *c.* 1705.

69 *(opposite above)* Four cards from a pack printed in Japan which reproduces national treasures kept at Ueno Museum.

70 *(opposite below)* Four cards from a pack illustrating bull-fighting published by Clemente Jacques y Cia of Mexico City in 1957.

The Queens Arms
n^th y^e New Motto

The Glorious Victory at Hochstet
wher^e y^e French and Bavarians
lost 40000 Men.

The Dredfull Storme
Nov y^e 26^ber 1703

The Taking Gibralter by
Sr Geo. Rook 24 Iuly
1704

73 Four cards from 'Events of the Reign of Queen Anne'.

74 *(opposite above)* King of spades from English fortune-telling pack (*c.* 1750).

75 *(opposite below)* 7 of diamonds from John Ogilby's geographical pack (1675).

somewhat bizarre group of noteworthies including King Arthur, Camber the third son of Brute, King of Cambria, Mary Stuart and Ossian, warrior and poet, son of Fingal, Knight of Ireland.

The seventeenth-century packs reflect, in their extreme one-sidedness and constant picturing of the dire penalties meted out to alleged enemies of the state, the almost hysterical nervousness of the British nation, their very real fear of Papal and Jesuitical intrigue. In a number of cards Jesuits or rebels are shown being hanged, sometimes in chains, sometimes five or six at a time; assassins are drawn to their execution, at least one lies prone on the scaffold preparatory to being quartered; Titus Oates is whipped at the cart-tail; peers are beheaded and the Popish Midwife, in three vivid cards, cuts up her husband, puts 'his quarters in ye Privy' (a family two-seater affair) and, very properly, as even Catholic husbands will think, burns at the stake. Most of the cards are somewhat coarsely executed, and it is interesting that those of the next century, when the country's feelings were not so closely involved and the hysteria had abated, reached higher standards of artistry as well as of impartiality. There are some enchanting and very lively little pictures in 'Events of the Reign of Queen Anne' [figure 73]. The ace of hearts announces 'Her M^ty Proclaim'd Q. of Eng. Scot. Fra. and Ireland &c March 8, 1701/2, another proclaims the new royal motto of *Semper Eadem,* and many of the cards commemorate, with vigorous battle scenes, the victories of Marlborough.

As the years went by, a sort of Academy of the Cards was created, providing self-study courses in a host of subjects. The

A man of pride, and favour'd of the great.
But much I doubt he'll know a lower state.

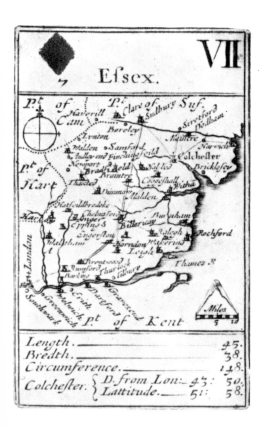

alphabet, arithmetic, anecdotes and aphorisms, astronomy, natural history, dance music, proverbs and mathematical instruments are some of the matters explained; but now we must leave them, forsaking education for diversion, learning for amusement.

Transformation cards, sometimes known as harlequin cards, are those in which the suit-signs have been altered, or transformed, either in the original engraved plate or on the finished card by pen and ink, so as to form part of a larger design. Some are delightful, most are ingenious and many aim, not always successfully, to amuse.

It has been suggested that the fashion, started by the prominent German publisher, Johann Friedrich, Freiherr Cotta von Cottendorf, Chancellor of the University of Tübingen, founder of the *Allgemeine Zeitung* and, with Schiller, *Die Horen*, and many other periodicals, was inspired by the annual almanacs which flourished in Germany and France at the time; certainly the publication of Cotta cards was an yearly event. He issued his first pack in 1805, when the court cards were figures taken from Schiller's play about Joan of Arc, *Die Jungfrau von Orleans*, and continued the series until 1811, with only one break, in 1809 [figures 79, 80, 84 and 87]. The idea was seized upon by cardmakers of others countries, resulting in the emergence of far more packs than can be described here. A few of the better known are mentioned.

In 1811 S. & J. Fuller, of The Temple of Fancy, Rathbone Place, London, published a pack with farcical figures mostly accompanied by a comical phrase or two, and for the most part poorly designed and executed. Between 1809 and 1819 Müller of Vienna issued three very handsome packs, which were engraved in stipple. In 1815 F. Osiander, who had designed for Cotta, continued the *Karten Almanach* with a pack in which Wellington, Blücher, Schwarzenberg and Kutusov take the place of the kings, and England, Russia, Prussia and Austria that of the queens. In 1819 Terquem & May of Paris brought out *Cartes Récréatives*. In 1828 E. Olivatte's work, modelled on Cotta, appeared in London, and in 1860 Reynolds and Sons of London issued cards transformed by T. S. Chapman. A Joan of Arc transformation pack was published in 1870 by Fromme und Bunte of Darmstadt. In 1879 Tiffany & Co. of New York published Harlequin Cards to the designs of C. E. Carryl, and in 1896 the United States Playing Card Co. published 'Vanity Fair No 41' [figure 82]. These, of course, were all printed packs, the earlier with hand-painted court cards, for sale in the normal way. In addition many packs were transformed by hand in pen-and-ink for personal or private amusement. Necessarily each such pack is unique, normally anonymous. Among individuals who have so amused themselves or their friends are Thackeray, with

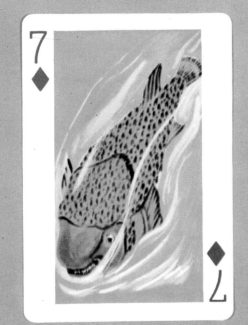

SCENOGRAPHIE
ou
ELEVATION

C'est l'aspect d'une place de guerre qui decouvre en pers: pective militaire les hauteurs de ses murailles et de ses terres, les profondeurs de ses fossez, son assiette et la forme de son enceinte

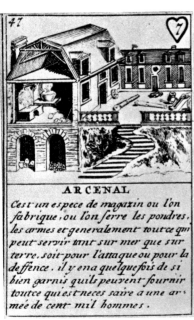

ARCENAL

C'est un espece de magazin ou l'on fabrique, ou l'on serre les poudres, les armes et generalement toutce qui peut servir tant sur mer que sur terre, soit pour l'attaque ou pour la deffence. il y en a quelquefois de si bien garnis quils peuvent fournir toutce qui est neces saire a une ar: mée de cent mil hommes.

77 8 of diamonds and 7 of hearts from *Jeu des Fortifications*, a companion pack to *Jeu de la Guerre* (c. 1710).

76 *(opposite)* Four cards from an Hawaiian souvenir pack.

twenty-one cards published in 'The Orphan of Pimlico', Count d'Orsay for the amusement of Lady Blessington, and Sir Edwin Landseer.

J. R. Planché, English playwright and Somerset Herald, remarks in the introduction to his *British Costume*, published in 1834, on the rapid spread, 'in recent years', of an interest in custume, adding: 'Its study, embellished by picture and enlivened by anecdote soon becomes interesting even to the young and careless reader.' The nineteenth-century card-makers clearly agreed with him, for many packs picturing clothes were created during the century. In particular O. Gibert and B. P. Grimaud, both of Paris, produced some splendid cards with the pasteboard kings and queens replaced by human monarchs, French and foreign, past and present, and British nobles, knights and countesses. They appear dressed in robes and ermine, tunics and tights, cloaks long and short, shoes pointed or buckled, gorgeous sweeping dresses with high upstanding collars and holding lovely fans, all delicately drawn, finely printed and beautifully hand-coloured [figure 42]. The French were not alone, however, in producing this type of card. Early in the century the American Jazaniah Ford printed a pack in honour of Decatur's victories in which the court figures wear Algerian costume, and this pack was later reprinted in honour of Lafayette's visit to America. Also early in the century a pack with figures of men and women in costumes of different classes was issued from Augsburg in Germany, and later another pack was produced for sale in Holland with Dutch men and women in national costume. In 1897 Charles Goodall & Co. Ltd printed a pack in honour of Queen Victoria's diamond jubilee with the court cards illustrative of English royal costume in Plantagenet, Tudor, Stuart and Hanoverian times [figure 10].

Divination and fortune-telling brought their own crop of cards quite apart from the Tarot, and also for that matter their own soothsayers, some of whom achieved notoriety. A Parisian *perruquier* of the eighteenth century who practised under the name of Etteilla – his own name, Alliette, backwards – , and Mme Lenormand, who claimed to have been consulted by Napoleon and Josephine, are perhaps the best known. Lenthall's cards of about 1670 are the earliest known fortune-telling pack. Generally the 'fortune' is printed at the foot of the cards, below little sketches illustrating the predestinarian phrase. The three of spades of a pack published in the middle of the nineteenth century depicts two horrified bathers watching two ruffians run off with their clothes, while the 'fortune' reads 'sudden losses will cause you some anxiety'. Cards with love mottos, in style very much the same as fortune-telling cards but, naturally, with different messages, also attained considerable popularity [figure 72]. The commemoration of notable events, wars (the Crimean,

89

THE BEGORRA BRIGADE.

THE ALDERMAN'S LUNCH.

A SPRING DAY.

78 Three Harlequin cards to the design of
C. E. Carryl and published by Tiffany & Co. of
New York in 1879.

Napoleonic, American Civil, Franco-Prussian and Russo-Japanese campaigns are examples), state events and royal occasions have all provided a most rich vein for mining by the card-makers. Souvenir cards with town or country scenes or pictures of a great exhibition have proved popular with visitors and profitable for their producers. The list could be stretched and stretched, for to card-making there seem to be neither bounds nor limit; but it is time to leave the past and turn to the present.

If twentieth-century card-makers have produced no great series of packs corresponding to, for example, the historical and transformation groups, they have printed many cards of original design. Photography, both black and white and coloured, has added another string to their bow. Satire and the celebration of great events, past and present, have continued to be sources of inspiration, while modern methods of publicity have provided fresh springs of fancy.

A pack satirizing religion was published in Russia about 1930. The court cards show priests and nuns indulging in scurrilous behaviour such as taking bribes or dreaming of a mistress whilst celebrating Mass, or imagining the embraces of a lover or the joys of the table whilst lighting votive candles [figure 59]. More recently the Social Democratic Party in Western Germany included in its propaganda a pack denigrating Dr Adenauer and his colleagues. It was suppressed.

To the designer bent on recording colourful events of the present, the English Royal Family, with five accessions, four coronations, a jubilee and many weddings, has provided much material [figure 10]. Among the interesting events of this century embalmed in playing cards is the progress of the Panama Canal, chronicled in two packs published by the United States Playing Card Co., one in 1908 and the other in 1915, which have on their foresides photographs of the principal features. Memorials to the past include two packs printed by the great Spanish firm of

Fournier, one honouring the centenary of the American Civil War, and one the discovery of the New World. The faces of the former display battle scenes and portraits of the leading personalities of the time, and those of the latter full-length figures of all the monarchs, explorers, navigators and conquistadors connected with the discovery of North and South America. This is a magnificent pack.

The Boer War made little impression on the card-makers, and is represented by only two packs, one for each side. Wüst of Frankfurt printed a pro-Boer pack with Kruger and General Cronje amongst the kings, while a second pack, roughly printed on coarse paper and with portraits of the English Royal Family in purple outline substituted for the usual card figures, was 'made by H. M. Guest, Klerksdorp, Transvaal, 1901, during the Anglo-Boer War' according to the announcement on the back [figure 85]. The circumstances in which the latter was created have been described, most kindly, in a letter dated 14 October 1966, by Colonel The Hon. Sir Lucas Guest, Rhodesian Minister of Air during the Second World War:

H. M. Guest of Klerksdorp was my Father. He came to Grahamstown, South Africa, with his parents from Kidderminster a hundred years ago last February. He was owner and editor of the Klerksdorp Mining Record, the only paper in the town. On the outbreak of the South African War he left Klerksdorp and returned as Reuter's Agent in 1901. The Guerilla warfare was at its height on his return. Mails were few and irregular and imported goods of any sort unobtainable. Considerable forces were operating in the district under Lord Methuen (incidentally I was a subaltern on his column). There was considerable demand for postcards, stationery and playing cards; but stocks were unobtainable. Father accordingly used his ingenuity, made the blocks with, I think, the help of an amateur carver friend, and printed the cards.

79, 80 *(above left and right)* 8 of hearts and 6 of clubs from Cotta's transformation pack of 1807.

81 *(below)* 4 of hearts transformed by T. S. Chapman and published by Reynolds in 1860.

The Great War, 1914–18, on the other hand, stirred the card-makers to abundant activity. Germany produced a quantity

91

82 Ace of hearts and knave of clubs from 'Vanity Fair No 41' published in 1896.

83 *(above right)* 'Mlle from Armentières' and others from an American pack printed in 1933.

84 *(opposite)* 6 of hearts, 7 of spades and 8 of diamonds from Cotta's transformation pack of 1811.

of well lithographed war packs with such eminent personages as the Kaiser, Hindenburg, Tirpitz and other leaders of the Triple Alliance in place of the usual court figures, and war scenes such as *'Sturm bei Ypern'* ('Storming Ypres') and *'Gefangene Franzosen'* ('French prisoners') on the pip cards. One of these packs was printed for Steinway & Sons, piano manufacturers, and distributed to the troops on their behalf. A tarot pack was printed by the famous firm of Piatnik u. Söhne of Vienna with the tarots dedicated to action; one, for instance, shows the destruction of an airship. On the Allied side, the United States produced four packs, one in 1915, one in 1917 and another in 1918, each with an ever more strident call to democracy ('Out with Kings and Queens!' and 'Keep the world safe for Democracy!' screamed accompanying publicity), and one long afterwards, in 1933, in commemoration of Armistice Day, 1918. The last, published by the Press of the Woolley Whale, had double-ended court cards with bemedalled generals and senior officers for kings, and junior officers and other ranks for knaves, while the queens were derived from the song 'Mademoiselle from Armentières'. The queens, whose names were blazoned on white sashes round their waists, were: clubs, Mlle from Orléans; spades, Mlle from Gay Paree; diamonds, Mlle from Andernach; and hearts, Mlle from Armentières [figure 83]. France, hampered by her laws forbidding deviation from the standard, issued two packs classed as *'Jeux d'Enfants'*, and therefore not subject to the same control as playing cards, which were printed on a single sheet, in one case 36 by 50 mm and in the other 140 by 190 mm. The latter

could be folded in the middle to form a letter card with the pack on the inside and the outsides free for the address and information. The court cards consisted of the President of France with 'Rép. Franç^se' as his queen, and allied kings and queens and marshals as the others, while the pip cards pictured various warlike subjects. The Montreal Lithograph Co. printed 'The Allied Armies', showing sovereigns and private soldiers of the Allies on the foresides and six national flags on the backs. England's contribution seems to have been restricted to five packs (three by Goodall & Son, two by Thomas de la Rue & Co.) with patriotic back designs.

During the Second World War, Van Mierle Proost of Brussels printed a pro-Allies pack which had sketches of Churchill, Roosevelt, Stalin and de Gaulle as kings, [figure 88], their consorts being four indeterminate women of whom the English is dressed in khaki and has a crown atop her 'tin hat', and three privates and a Cossack as knaves. On the aces are outlines of Big Ben, the Statue of Liberty, the Eiffel Tower and the Kremlin. Prisoners-of-war made their own cards, and Herr Janssen in his book *Speelkaarten* describes a pack made in Buchenwald concentration camp by a Czech journalist from cigarette packets. In October 1966 The Red Rabbit, the well-known American dealer, offered a 'complete set of rare hand-carved hand-painted bone playing cards by prisoner of war and also bone dominoes, in bone inlaid box, 1 bone die and spinner'.

In a conglomerate group we find actors and actreses of the nineteen-twenties replacing the kings and queens; two Icelandic packs, one based on mythological tradition and one on the Icelandic way of life; bull-fighting packs published by Fournier;

85 Court cards (the same for each suit) and the 'No Joker' produced in conditions of scarcity during the Boer War by H. M. Guest in 1901.

mythological and bull-fighting packs by the noted business of
Clemente Jacques y Cia of Mexico City [figure 70]; 'Florentine',
printed by Draeger Frères of Paris from miniatures painted by
Émile Bécat for Les Éditions Philibert, double-ended and displaying scantily clad or naked ladies in the arms of their com-
panions (and sometimes the other way round) and more closely
involved one way up than the other [figure 36]; and a medical
pack produced by the United States Playing Card Co. for the
Schering Foundation to honour the medical professions in which
young doctors, nurses, chemists and research workers appear in
white gowns and masks with stethoscopes, pills and similar
equipment.

Several attempts have been made to break with tradition, to
induce the public to accept cards in easily recognized but
different and freshly conceived contemporary decorative
patterns. About 1930, the New York Card Co. manufactured a
pack with large pips and court cards with Burne-Jones-like
figures in early English robes tinted with an unusual amount of
green and purple. In 1955 the Miro Company of Paris printed a
Canasta pack in which the clothing of the court cards is drawn
mainly with straight lines and the suit-signs form a major part of
their embellishment. In 1957, the De la Rue Co. promoted a
competition, open to designers of all countries, for a new imagery
which would yet leave signs and figures easily recognizable. The
prize was won by a French artist, Jean Picart le Doux. Though
cards of beauty were printed from the prize-winning drawings,
the pack met with the same fate as all other attempts at originality
– commercial failure.

Card faces different in their entirety, as opposed to con-

86 *(above)* Knave of clubs, queen of hearts and
knave of spades from a pro-Allies pack printed in
Belgium during the First World War.

87 *(below)* 5 of spades from Cotta's transformation
pack of 1807.

95

temporary adaptation, have been devised by South Africa and the United States, though for reasons quite different from the simple desire to make a change. On leaving the Commonwealth, South Africa decided to republicanize her cards along with her politics, and created a pack, Boer in character, from which all traces of monarchy have been excluded. The suits become cartwheels, tent-pegs, shoes and powder-horns, and the court cards *Boer*, *Vrou* and *Kommandant*; *President* replaces the ace [figure

88 The four kings and a joker from a pro-Allies pack printed in Belgium during the Second World War.

89]. The United States has marketed a variety of souvenir packs consisting only of coloured photographs with indices added to the corners. Although beautiful and undoubtedly playing cards, since they can be used for gaming, it is difficult to accept them alongside packs of a more customary flavour.

The high standard of modern printing and photography, together with modern advertising methods and the public's refusal to accept new face designs as anything but ephemera, has diverted the card manufacturer's energy and ingenuity into the creation of imaginative, attractive and splendidly printed back designs. In recent years they have appeared in their thousands, some on standard, some on advertising packs, and a collection can easily exceed twenty thousand.

In these pages a very brief look has been taken at the long and varied life of playing cards, during which they have changed from the limited work of gifted artists to the multiple product of impersonal machinery. They have brought, and still bring, much pleasure, easement of boredom and relief of tension to an ever-increasing multitude of people throughout the world. Such a long continuing service to mankind surely deserves a respectful salute.

89 The *Vrou* (queen) of cartwheels and *Boer* (knave) of powder-horns from a South African pack designed after the establishment of the Republic.